T0330521

The Economics of
Cooperative Education

A considerable number of higher educational institutions in North America, Oceania, and Europe, offer what are known as cooperative education, work-integrated learning, work placements, sandwich courses, or internships, to provide pragmatic experience to students, and its popularity is spreading to many higher educational institutions in the world. Alongside such development, the rising need for theoretical research and objective assessment are felt among those academics and practitioners involved in these programmes.

The book offers a rigorous theoretical framework based on the human capital theory of labour economics and econometric analysis, which are well-established concepts in the field of economics, with an objective quantitative methodology to analyse and assess cooperative education programmes.

Yasushi Tanaka is Professor in the Faculty of Economics at Kyoto Sangyo University, Kyoto, Japan. His main research field is labour economics. He is also a member of the steering committee of the Center of Research and Development for Cooperative Education (CRDCE) at Kyoto Sangyo University, and a member of the World Association of Cooperative Education (WACE) Commission on Strategic Planning as well as of the WACE International Research Group.

Routledge Studies in the Modern World Economy

The Economics of Cooperative Education

A practitioners' guide to the theoretical
framework and empirical assessment
of cooperative education

Yasushi Tanaka

Routledge
Taylor & Francis Group

LONDON AND NEW YORK

First published 2015
by Routledge
2 Park Square, Milton Park, Abingdon, Oxon OX14 4RN

and by Routledge
711 Third Avenue, New York, NY 10017

Routledge is an imprint of the Taylor & Francis Group, an informa business

© 2015 Yasushi Tanaka

British Library Cataloguing in Publication Data
A catalogue record for this book is available from the British Library

Library of Congress Cataloging-in-Publication Data
A catalog record for this book has been requested.

ISBN: 978-0-415-63887-6 (hbk)
ISBN: 978-1-315-74627-2 (ebk)

Typeset in Galliard
by Apex CoVantage, LLC

Contents

Tables

Figures

Acknowledgements

I would like to express my sincere gratitude to Professor Yusaku Kataoka for advising me on the theoretical framework for quantitative analysis, Professor Emeritus Fumihiko Goto and Mr Masaaki Nakagawa for initially introducing me to the world of cooperative education from Kyoto Sangyo University, Dr Paul Stonely, the CEO of the World Association of Cooperative Education, and Ms Keiko Miyakawa, its Japan representative for providing the opportunity to present my ideas at WACE conferences and the referees and participants at the conferences who made many useful comments and suggestions to my papers, the staff at the KSU Center of Research and Development for Co-operative Education for kindly supplying the KSU data for the quantitative investigation of the book, and Ms Yongling Lam and Ms Deepti Agarwal from the editorial team.

Lastly, I would like to add to the list my family—my wife Maricruz, and my children Masumi, and Yasushi-Xavier, who gave me constant spiritual support throughout the publication process.

1 Introduction

Cooperative education has been spreading among the industrialized countries since its birth in early 20th century America. This educational system of "connecting study and work" has become an important experience particularly for job-seeking graduates in these countries. It is more so as the income rises and the demand for higher education rises as a consequence. *Education at Glance,* a publication by the Organisation for Economic Co-operation and Development (OECD), provides the trend in the percentage of graduates of tertiary education among the youth population, and the figures show a gradual but definite increase in the percentage. According to OECD (2013), between 1995 and 2011, the OECD average for entry rates at tertiary educational institutions for a tertiary-type A education defined as theory-based programme with a duration of at least three years has risen from 39 per cent to 60 per cent. With the increase in the number of graduates, they are no longer the elites of working population to lead their industrial societies. Rather, with high quality, they are beginning to constitute the main body of the working population. More graduates, however, implies a more intensifying competition for jobs among them and cooperative education as credential may add an extra value to their CVs. For employers, employing graduates with cooperative education experience can reduce their on-the-job training costs. For educational institutions, providing such opportunities to students can help maintaining their competitive edge in the market for higher education. Therefore, cooperative education can conveniently fit into this gap created by socioeconomic change to serve the stakeholders of the system of higher education – students, industry, and educational institutions.

The form of cooperative education varies by social background of the country, and its effectiveness depends on the economic environment the country is in. Presently, among the industrialized countries, cooperative education in higher education has been more developed in North America, Oceania, and Northern Europe, with many Asian counterparts still falling behind. On the whole, it is fair to say that cooperative education still has some way to go before establishing itself as one of the main systems of education.

I am myself a late comer into this multidisciplinary field, where constant devotion and the enthusiasm of the practitioners and researchers were much felt. As an economist by training, however, I also felt slightly uncomfortable that quantitative research was not commonly pursued. There is no doubt that presenting objective data based on logical conceptualization will supplement the effort of the practitioners and researchers to earn support from the university administration, other academic staffs, as well as industry and government for further development. Thus this book attempts to provide these two tools, that is, theoretical framework and empirical assessment.

The first is its theoretical framework – or how cooperative education fits into the main frame educational system and what it offers to graduates and employers. Cooperative education has often been analysed from educational theory perspectives. Its analysis seems to emphasize the educational aspect of cooperative education. This book attempts to apply an approach from labour economics to explain how cooperative education contributes to work, productivity, and earnings, by using the concepts of Human Capital Theory and Screening/Signalling Theory. Surprisingly, there is no explicit analysis on cooperative education in labour economics literature nor cooperative education literature dealing with labour economics.

The second is its empirical assessment – how we can know if any cooperative education programme is worthwhile. There is no doubt that cooperative education has a positive effect on educational development of a student. But to what degree? Education is generally labour intensive and thus costly activity, and it is necessary for any educational programme to clarify its effectiveness to justify its raison d'être. This book summarizes statistical/econometric tools to quantitatively assess the effect of cooperative education programmes. This is done through illustrating by examples how to choose and analyse data for cooperative education at a given educational institution.

The book is divided into three parts. Part I gives a brief introduction of cooperative education as a background for the theoretical and empirical analyses to follow. Chapter 1 deals with the history, present state, and definition of cooperative education. The history follows the American history of cooperative education since 1906, when Herman Schneider started cooperative system of education programme at University of Cincinnati and throughout its development in the 20th century. The present state discusses how it is operating in some of the countries where cooperative education is well-established, that is, Canada, Australia, and the United Kingdom, although the concept has different names among these countries. Finally, various concepts of cooperative education are discussed and an attempt is made to redefine the concept. It is important to clarify what is meant by cooperative education for the remaining sections of the book.

Part II deals with the theoretical framework of cooperative education. As stated above, very little has been discussed about cooperative education in economics and labour economics in particular. Labour economics analyses the effects on productivity and wage of academic study at educational institution and on-the-job training at workplace but not of cooperative education, which occurs in both places. This book argues that cooperative education supplements both education and on-the-job training. In order to support this premise,

Chapter 3 introduces Human Capital Theory. This theory of investment in education tells us why and to what degree education is economically worthwhile. Chapter 3 also introduces another function of education based on Screening/ Signalling Theory. This theory tells us education acts as a credential to prove the student's ability. These concepts are employed in Chapter 4 to explain the economic function of cooperative education and applied to analyse how cooperative education could develop in a country where it is still little known but could play a major role in near future with Japan as an example.

Part III deals with empirical assessment of the effectiveness of cooperative education programme. Various statistical/econometric tools are introduced and applied to analyse real cases. Chapter 5 offers the analytical framework to assess the effectiveness of cooperative education, and some of the few past studies are illustrated with a brief survey. Chapter 6 deals with statistical tests and shows how these are used to compare means and proportions of two groups. After solving simple examples for a t test, a z test, a χ^2 test, and analysis of variance (ANOVA), the students' data from Kyoto Sangyo University (KSU) are used to verify the effect of cooperative education with these tests.

For Chapters 7, 8, 9, and 10, the analysis is based on econometric analysis of multiple regression in which EVIEWS was used for the calculation. Chapter 7 provides the analytical framework based on path analysis and the six hypotheses to be tested in the following chapters. Chapter 8 examines if cooperative education is taken by already academically motivated students using data collected from all students graduated from KSU in 2008 and 2009. Chapter 9 investigates the effect of cooperative education on academic performance. This is done by two ways. One is based on KSU data and the other is an international comparison between KSU and Hong Kong Polytechnic University (PolyU). In Chapter 10, the effect of cooperative education on employment outcome is analysed by looking at the employment status of the first job and first company, as well as alumni's job performance based on questionnaires. Finally, Chapter 11 concludes with a summary of what has been established and the limitations, as well as suggestions for further investigations.

The book should be accessible to practitioners of cooperative education without advanced knowledge of economic theory, statistics, or econometrics. The main purpose of this book is to help the busy cooperative education practitioners to conduct the empirical investigation without having to read a whole book of statistics, econometrics, or economic theory. For that reason, I have made the explanations as compact as possible but providing reference for those wishing to know more about the theoretical background. Furthermore, it is emphasized, however, is that the theoretical and empirical concepts used from these fields are fully understood through numerical examples.

This is not to deny a series of existing approaches to analyse the effectiveness of cooperative education including those based on educational theory, psychology, or any other qualitative analysis. On the contrary, it is hoped that our approach supplements rather than replaces other existing approaches in support of practitioners and researchers of cooperative education.

Part I
The background

2 History, present state, and definition of cooperative education

(1) The history of cooperative education – its birth in the United States

It is generally understood by researchers and practitioners of cooperative education that this educational system was initiated by Herman Schneider in 1906 at the University of Cincinnati, United States (The development of the concept of cooperative education by Schneider is well documented in Ryder (1987)). Although Schneider himself stated that this form of educational system where study and work are connected had long been employed within the fields of law and medicine, it is probably correct to say that he created cooperative education as a well-structured system of education. On 26th of January 1914, Herman Schneider was summoned to the hearings of Committee on Education of the House of Representatives during the Sixty-Third Congress of the United States of America. The dean of the College of Engineering of the University of Cincinnati explained that with the cooperative system of education,

> [t]he theoretical work in the university and the practical work in the commercial field are coordinated by a number of devices, but principally by the use of teachers whom we call coordinators. Every afternoon these coordinators, who are either professors or instructors, are out where the students are at work observing all the details of operations involved, and taking notes that will enable them to use the practical experience of the students in their theoretical instruction. . . . [T]he theory and practice are made to work hand in hand so that the practical work has the highest possible educational value.
>
> (Committee on Education, House of Representatives, Sixty-Third Congress, United States of America, 1914)

In 1909, the Polytechinic School of the YMCA Evening Institute (now Northeastern University) followed the University of Cincinnati to introduce cooperative education for engineering students, both of whom are known to be the pioneers to this day. In 1926, the Association of Cooperative colleges was formed with Schneider as the president. The Association succeeded in 1929 to set up the Division of Cooperative Engineering Education within the Society for the Promotion of Engineering Education.

Since 1906, cooperative education had been developed mainly for engineering students. But in 1919, the University of Cincinnati launched cooperative education for business students, while in 1921, Antioch College offered cooperative education to students of liberal arts. By 1941, 39 educational institutions were offering cooperative education in the United States. Despite its drop during the World War II, the number picked up to record about 60 institutions by 1956.

It goes without saying that support from industry is indispensable for the development of this programme. In 1957, the Edison Foundation financed a conference to assess cooperative education's potential in higher education. In 1961, a book titled *Work-Study College Program* (Wilson and Lyon, 1961) was published to assess the value of cooperative education, which had funding support of the Ford Foundation Fund for the Advancement of Education. In 1962, the National Commission for Cooperative Education (NCCE) was incorporated with college presidents as its board members. The purpose of NCCE was to nationally promote cooperative education and appeal the US government for funds. In 1963, the National Cooperative Education Association (NCEA) (now the Cooperative Education and Internship Association [CEIA]) was set up to promote cooperative education among educational institutions with its memberships open to individuals as well as organizations. The US government responded by offering the funding with the Higher Education Act of 1965, which was further strengthened with the title VIII of the Amendment of 1968. According to the Cooperative Education Research Center of Northeastern University, in 1971, there were 277 universities and colleges offering cooperative education, and in 1986, the number grew to 1,012, approximately a third of all the higher educational institutions in the United States (Sovilla and Varty, 2011). Alongside this growth, the government funding rose to $4.5 million in 1971 and 1972, and reached $10 million in 1973. It needs to be mentioned, however, that such a rapid growth in quantity was made possible partly due to somewhat enlarged interpretation of the concept by the government, which consequently brought down its quality (For more detailed explanations on the trend of cooperative eudcation in the US, see Wilson (1987)).

There were other factors that brought about the rapid growth in number. One is the fast technological advancement of the post-war period. This required a large number of newly skilled workers, and yet companies were lacking time and money to prepare this young labour force. This was where universities and colleges could serve by providing work experience while they studied.

Another is the introduction of cooperative education at community colleges. Unlike the standard cooperative education programmes in universities and colleges where students study and work alternately over a period of academic programme, community colleges offered programmes where study hours and work hours are set within a day. This system helped to provide students with financial difficulty an opportunity to study. The increase of tuition fees at that time further increased the value of such a cooperative education programme, and this led to the idea of including cooperative education within the mainstream of higher education programme as a creditable programme. The consequence of such a trend was that cooperative education needed to be modified to satisfy the requirements of orthodox academic courses, making it *a small and highly supervised programme for what were viewed as privileged high-achieving students* (Wooldridge, 1987, 24). This is not in line with how Schneider thought cooperative education should be, as stated in the hearings of Committee on Education of the House of Representatives during the Sixty-Third Congress of the United States of America in 1914:

> [The majority of his] students could not take the college course were it not for the money they earn in the course. . . . Many more boys continue in school under the cooperative system, because of the opportunity to do half-time work, to learn a trade, and to get a supplementary schooling. Nearly all of these boys would have gone to work full time.

The government funding for cooperative education that started with the Higher Education Act of 1965 effectively ended in 1996 following the introduction of the Amendment of 1992 (Title VIII Cooperative education). According to NCCE, the number of institutions offering cooperative education fell to around 400, less than a half of the peak in 1986. This seems to suggest that government financial support played an important role for running of cooperative education programmes. Given the present economic situation that government funding may be hard to come by, universities need to find cost-effective ways to manage cooperative education programmes. And this does apply to universities in other countries, too.

(2) The present state of cooperative education – the rest of the world

Cooperative education has been spread outside the United States, particularly among English-speaking countries such as Canada, Australia, New Zealand, the United Kingdom, and South Africa, although the naming and style of the programme differ among them. Each of these countries has its own national association for cooperative education that hosts research seminars and conferences on a regular basis, promotes the concept, and provides the quality assurance for the existing programmes.

The following are some of national associations in operation:

United States	Cooperative Education and Internship Association (CEIA)
Canada	Canadian Association for Co-operative Education (CAFCE)
United Kingdom	Association for Sandwich Education and Training (ASET)
Australia	Australian Collaborative Education Network (ACEN)
New Zealand	New Zealand Association for Cooperative Education (NZACE)

South Africa	South African Society for Cooperative Education (SASCE)
Thailand	Thai Association for Cooperative Education (TACE)
Sweden	The Vilar Network

In 1983, The World Council and Assembly on Cooperative Education was founded to foster cooperative education worldwide with college and university presidents, educational specialists and employers from Australia, Canada, Hong Kong, the Netherlands, the Philippines, the United States, and the United Kingdom. In 1991, it was renamed as the World Association for Cooperative Education (WACE), and it has been hosting international conferences and symposiums regularly. WACE has been working to promote collaborations among the national associations – the national associations in the above list participate regularly in the national associations meeting held during the WACE conferences, as well as to promote the concept among those countries where cooperative education is not well established.

Among these countries, Canada, Australia, and the United Kingdom have well-established cooperative education systems, although their names vary among countries and even among educational institutions within in the same country – either because each institution started the programme from its own background and policy or because each is keen to differentiate its programme from the rest. The cooperative education systems in these three countries are described briefly below (see Turner and Frederick (1987) for more countries).

(i) Canada

Cooperative education in Canada started at the University of Waterloo in 1957 about a half century behind the United States. As in the United States, the popularity grew particularly with an introduction of cooperative education to community colleges in 1960s. CAFCE, the national association for cooperative education of Canada, was founded in 1973 and had 83 member institutions in 2013 (www.cafce.ca). Among the Canadian universities, the University of Waterloo claims to have the world's largest co-op program with approximately 16,500 undergraduate co-op students, and to have 4,500 regularly participating co-op employers in 2013 (http://uwaterloo.ca/co-operative-education/). In the State of British Columbia, University of British Columbia offered over 2,900 placements in arts, commerce, engineering, forestry, kinesiology, and science in 2009 (www.coop.ubc.ca), while the figure at the at the University of Victoria shows the university offered over 2,800 placements in 2011 according to its Co-operative Education and Career Services.

(ii) Australia

The first cooperative education in Australia was launched at Victoria University and Swinburne University of Technology in 1963. The national association for cooperative education, the Australian Cooperative Education Society (ACES) was founded in 1990 but failed to sustain itself. Since 2006, ACEN has been taking its role as the national association with 36 member institutions as of 2013. Instead of using the term *cooperative education,* ACEN refers to the work-integrated learning (WIL) as the overall concept, which includes internships, cooperative education, work placements, industrial learning, community based learning, clinical rotations, sandwich year, and practical projects (http://acen.edu.au/). The possible reason why the term cooperative education is not used is due to the confusion that might arise with the Robert Owen's cooperative movement and various cooperatives that exist today such as worker's cooperatives and consumer's cooperatives. Of the two pioneer universities of cooperative education in Australia, Victoria University offers the programmes under the titles of "placements" and "work integrated learning for business students," and it introduced a policy in 2010 to mandate that a minimum of 25 per cent of programme content and assessment must be related to WIL (Venables et al., 2009). Swinburne University of Technology, the other pioneer, runs what they call Industry Engaged Learning, which is defined as a learning process also sometimes referred to as work-integrated learning, cooperative education, or work based learning (www.swinburne.edu.au/iel/). Patrick and Kay (2011) offers an overall picture of the subject.

(iii)   The United Kingdom

A similar system to cooperative education known as a sandwich course started in 1903 at Sunderland Technical College (now the University of Sunderland). Prior to this, in 1823, George Birkbeck started an educational institution for working people offering part-time courses in London, which later was named Birkbeck college (now Birkbeck, University of London). Although they both dealt with a work and study programme, the former type provided opportunity to work for students, while the latter provided opportunity to study for working people or adult education (See Billet and Choy (2011)). A typical sandwich course also known as "a placement year" would "sandwich" a year of work experience, also known as "a placement year" between second and third years of a three-year undergraduate programme, making it a four-year programme. In the United Kingdom, universities and polytechnics coexisted as the institutions of higher education, where the former tended to emphasize research and theoretical teaching, while the latter tended to emphasize more practical teaching. Similar to the American counterpart, the sandwich course had been more common among engineering degrees and in polytechnics. With the Further and Higher Education Act 1992, polytechnics are now called universities, but their tendency of offering sandwich courses still remains.

ASET was formed in 1979 as the national association to take care of sandwich courses. Today, it has 112 members who are mostly educational institutions by 2014 and in line with the global trend in cooperative education, it states as its mission a promotion of the concept of "integrated work-based and placement learning" (www.asetonline.org/index.htm). Among the former universities, Aston University and the University of Surrey are known to have established placement programmes. By 2013, at Aston University, around 70 per cent of

Table 2-1 The summary of development of cooperative education

A. The origin of cooperative education

   1906   Herman Schneider to start cooperative education for engineering students at University of Cincinnati

   1909   Northeastern University to start cooperative education for engineering students

   1926   Association of Cooperative Colleges formed with H. Schneider as president

   1929   Division of Cooperative Engineering Education (DCEE) (now called Cooperative and Experiential Education Division, CEED) set up at Society for Promotion of Engineering Education (SPEE) (now called American Society for Engineering Education [ASEE])

B. Expansion to other fields

   1919   University of Cincinnati to start cooperative education programme in business

   1921   Antioch College to start cooperative education programme in liberal arts

C. National associations and industrial support

   1957   Edison foundation to hold a conference on cooperative education

   1961   Ford Foundation Fund for the Advancement of Education to support a publication of a book *Work-Study College Programs*

   1962   National Commission for Cooperative Education (NCCE) incorporated, to promote cooperative education and to raise federal government funding

   1963   National Cooperative Education Association (NCEA) incorporated (now Cooperative Education and Internship Association [CEIA])

D. Federal support

   1965   Higher Education Act of 1965 under President Lyndon Johnson for funding institutions for establishing and expanding of cooperative education

   1968   Title VIII of the Amendment of 1968 for further support

   1992   Amendment of 1992 to effectively end support by 1996

   (Government funding in 1970s)

1971	1972	1973	1985
$4.5m	$4.5m	$10m	$14m

E. A number of institutions offering cooperative edeucation programme

1941	1956	1971	1986	1996
39	60	277	1012	400~450

F. Development in Canada, Australia, the United Kingdom, and the world (UK)

   1823   Birkbeck to start education for working people

   1903   University of Sunderland to start a sandwich course

   1979   ASET formed

(Canada)

1957 University of Waterloo to start cooperative education

1973 CAFCE formed

(Australia)

1963 Victoria University and Swinburne University to start cooperative education

2006 ACEN formed

(World)

1983 World Council and Assembly on Cooperative Education formed

1991 Renamed as World Association for Cooperative Education (WACE)

2010 WACE merged with NCCE

the undergraduate students take a placement year or language year abroad (www1. aston.ac.uk/ undergraduate/placements/), while at the University of Surrey, the programme is termed as professional training, which is described as a similar concept to work-based learning, work-integrated learning, co-operative education, industry-based learning, and collaborative learning, over 50 per cent of the students choose to do the placement (www.surrey.ac.uk/professionaltraining).

(3) Definition of cooperative education

As has been seen, various terms exist to express this type of work and study programme apart from cooperative education, and this sometimes causes confusion. The confusion is exacerbated by the fact that there is no single and clear definition of the concept at hand. Consequently, many educational institutions use their own terms to express what amounts to be cooperative education. This section introduces these terms that are frequently used in the literature by academics as well as practitioners, in order to clarify the similarities and differences among them. It is important for the theoretical and empirical analysis in the following chapters to understand clearly first what is meant by cooperative education (See Groenewald et al (2011) for a systematic approach).

(i) *Cooperative education (or co-op education or coop)*

The basic features of cooperative education still remain unchanged after a century of its development since Schneider's explanation during the hearings of Committee on Education of the House of Representatives during the Sixty-Third Congress of the United States of America that with the cooperative system of education,

> [t]he theoretical work in the university and the practical work in the commercial field are coordinated by a number of devices, but principally by the use of teachers whom we call coordinators. . . . [T]he theory and practice

are made to work hand in hand so that the practical work has the highest possible educational value.

A similar definition is given by, for example, by CAFCE, the Canadian national association for cooperative education:

"Co-operative Education Program" means a program which alternates periods of academic study with periods of work experience in appropriate fields of business, industry, government, social services and the professions in accordance with the following criteria:

  (i) each work situation is developed and/or approved by the co-operative educational institution as a suitable learning situation;
 (ii) the co-operative student is engaged in productive work rather than merely observing;
(iii) the co-operative student receives remuneration for the work performed;
 (iv) the co-operative student's progress on the job is monitored by the co-operative educational institution;
  (v) the co-operative student's performance on the job is supervised and evaluated by the student's co-operative employer;
 (vi) the time spent in periods of work experience must be at least thirty per cent of the time spent in academic study.

The CAFCE's definition is more specific about the roles of educational institutions and of employers, than, but consistent with, the original version of cooperative education advocated by Schneider. As mentioned earlier, the national associations of cooperative education have been working closely and sharing ideas particularly through the WACE conferences and symposiums. The concept of cooperative education is well-shared worldwide and the CAFCE's definition may represent the standard definition. However, there are at least three such aspects that vary among the countries. First is the non-credit nature of cooperative education, which even varies among the institutions within a country. Some consider it to be a requirement for graduation – even in this case, some counts cooperative education within academic credits while others keep it outside, while others provide a certificate of completion upon graduation as an option. Second is the duration of work experience. In most of cases, they are between 6 and 12 months and with more than one employer. Third is the payment. Some may accept volunteer activities as the part of work-study programme.

For the purpose of theoretical and empirical analyses to follow, a slightly modified version of the CAFCE's definition will be used as the definition of cooperative education by eliminating the specific length of duration of work experience (i.e. [vi]) and summarizing the criteria by the three stakeholders, that is, educational institution, student, and employer, to create a more general definition of cooperative education:

"Cooperative Education" is an integrated educational programme of on-campus academic study and related off-campus work experience offered at higher educational institution, which satisfies following criteria:

(i) *the cooperative educational institution* develops and/or approves the off-campus work experience suitable for cooperative education learning, and monitors the student's progress during the period of work experience.
(ii) *the cooperative education student* is engaged in productive activity rather than merely work observation during the work experience, and receives remuneration for the activity.
(iii) *the cooperative education employer* supervises and evaluates student's performance during the activity.

In short, cooperative education is defined as an on-campus and off-campus educational system that involves a higher educational institution and an employer, where the co-op students are paid for the off-campus work experience. And the decision is left to each institution to determine whether it may or may not be counted as academic credit towards graduation. As for the duration of the off-campus work experience, although not clearly stated, a minimum of three months may be required – it is what a WACE certificate titled "Students Achievement Award for International Work Experience" quotes. It seems reasonable, since WACE would set up a standard that is globally acceptable.

(ii) Internship

Because there is no clear definition for cooperative education itself as explained, it is difficult to talk about the exact distinction between the two terms. In fact, here are educational institutions that offer the two programmes, implying in this case the two are distinguishable. The University of Cincinnati is one of such educational institutions. At the University of Cincinnati, the Division of Professional Practice takes care of the Cooperative Education Program and the Academic Internship Program. On the title pages of the division, it states, "Coop = Experience + Cash for College" and "Internship = Experience + Flexible Scheduling" (www.uc.edu/prppractice.html). The former emphasizes terms of full-time classes and full-time work alternating, where classes are fully integrated in the academic programme, and work provides a salary. The latter, in contrast, emphasizes that the relation is between a student and an employer, although the university can provide academic support pre- and post-internship programmes. The distinction, however, becomes less apparent with their Academic Internship Program, which seems to have more university involvement.

It can be safely said that internships are in general less academic and more work oriented and have less of quality assurance involvement by educational institutions. It is also important to point out that in many cases internees are not paid a salary. Perlin (2011) points out that many internees are used by their employers for the purpose of cutting cost. Interestingly, while Perlin (2011) is rather critical about internships, in which the internees often work with no wage or below the legal minimum wage without labour protection, he sees cooperative education as providing the ideal relationship among the stakeholders: a student, an employer, and an educational institution. Clearly, internship does not satisfy our definition of cooperative education.

(iii)   Sandwich course

As explained earlier in case of the United Kingdom, it is an alternative form of cooperative education. The main difference is that the work experience, or often labelled as "placement," is for a year and remunerable, being sandwiched between the second and third years, while a typical North American cooperative education programme spreads 12-month work experience over entire undergraduate years, particularly using summer terms with different employers. Other terms, such as professional practices, may be used in the United Kingdom, but it is clear that the concept satisfies our definition of cooperative education.

(iv)   Apprenticeship

Like the sandwich course mentioned above, apprenticeship is a system that involves a school leaver (or a graduate) with a new job through on-the-job training. It is a system with a long history, and there is a relatively large volume of research within the field of economics, including its effect on employment possibility and wages. (See, for example, an extensive survey in Ryan, (2001), in which the situation of transition from school to work is compared among seven industrial countries). However, it differs from cooperative education in the following three aspects: (1) the main focus of this research is on the leavers of secondary education and not the graduates of higher education; (2) the skills to be acquired are hard skills rather than soft skills; (3) the programme is organized by an employer rather than a higher education institution.

Therefore, apprenticeship needs to be distinguished from cooperative education.

(v)   Work-integrated learning (WIL) / Work-integrated education (WIE) / Work-based learning (WBL)

These terms are used almost interchangeably. Increasingly, they are used to supplement the term cooperative education among academics and practitioners of cooperative education in conferences.

WACE, for example, recently introduced the term "Cooperative & Work-Integrated Education (CWIE)" as a subtitle in the logo. They define CWIE as a concept that includes all forms of experiential learning such as cooperative education, internships, semester in industry, international co-op exchanges, study abroad, research, clinical rotations, service learning, and community services (www.waceinc.org). In other words, it is a learning process through interactions between classroom and non-classroom activities with the latter not necessarily being a paid work activity. Thus, our definition of cooperative education is one form of WIL, WIE, and WBL, and not their synonym.

It needs to be mentioned that the term *learning* is also used as in "learning in life" or "lifelong learning," in which the learning space is not confined to educational institutions. WIL and WBL in the present context exclude such a case.

(vi)   Project-based learning (PBL)

The concept of PBL can be traced as far back as the beginning of 20th century with the work of John Dewey, an American educator and philosopher (Dewey, 1916). It is an educational programme of personal development though engagement in projects dealing with real-world problems. It is a study-through-experience programme, in which the experience is pursued through working on a project in a classroom. The effectiveness of PBL on academic performance has been found with the students in PBL classrooms getting higher scores than those in traditional classrooms. (As an introduction of PBL to those who are not familiar with the concept, see Krajcik and Blumenfeld (2006)).

In its essence, however, it is an educational programme and not a work study programme that is our primary concern. The work experience is given by an employer on campus as a project rather than at the workplace, unlike an orthodox cooperative education programmes. It differs from cooperative education also because a project may be carried out by a group of students, so that a university and an employer can supervise more than one student. This makes it easier for both the university and the coop employer since it is less time consuming than one-to-one supervision of an orthodox cooperative education programme. Also, the university requires less coop employers, while the coop employer too needs not provide a permanent space for the coop students during the work experience. To include PBL in the mainstream of cooperative education as defined in this book, however, would require clarification of the length of the project period as well as of remuneration. So this is not cooperative education in the strict sense.

(vii)   Experiential learning

Experiential learning is a well-established concept in the field of psychology. Kolb (1984) defined experiential learning as "the process whereby knowledge is created through the transformation of experience." Furthermore, he developed his own interpretation of experiential learning from three models of the experiential learning process: Dewey's model of learning (Dewey, 1938), Lewin's model of action research and laboratory (Lewin, 1946), and Piaget's model of learning and cognitive development (Piaget, 1985). Kolb introduced a concept of circular learning process, or what is also known as the Kolb Cycle with four phases:

> (Phase 1: Concrete experience)
>> Learners involve themselves fully, openly, and without bias in new experiences.
>
> (Phase 2: Reflective observation)
>> They must be able to reflect on and observe their experiences from many perspectives.
>
> (Phase 3: Abstract conceptualization)
>> They must be able to create concepts that integrate their observations into logically sound theories.
>
> (Phase 4: Active experimentation)
>> They must be able to use these theories to make decisions and solve problems.

And back to Phase 1

There is a large volume of literature on experiential learning, particularly around the works of Dewey, Lewin, Piaget, and Kolb in social psychology, and its application to cooperative education may be found in Eames and Cates (2011). Like WIL, WIE, and WBL, experiential learning is an umbrella term to include learning process with experience. Consequently, cooperative education as defined in (i) is not equivalent to but one specific type of experiential learning.

This chapter has provided a brief introduction of cooperative education – how it started, how it is managed, and how it should be defined. Needless to say, there is a huge volume of literature in these aspects of cooperative education. Interested readers should be referred to other sources for much closer examination of these areas, since the aim of this chapter is not an extensive examination of cooperative education but to provide a background for the theoretical and empirical aspects of the concept. As for this book, the discussion will now proceed to an economic analysis of cooperative education.

Part II

The theoretical framework: an economic analysis of cooperative education

3 Investing in human capital
Education and on-the-job training

It is customary in economic analysis to divide consumer's action into "consuming today" and "saving today for consuming tomorrow." The savings could be utilized for financing business through banks, and issuing of shares and bonds, until they are cashed for the future consumption. This is the concept of investment in which "capital" is formed for future production. A similar line of argument may be made for one's decision to receive education: "One reduces consumption to save in order to pay for education today, to form 'human capital' to raise his or her productive ability tomorrow." The basic concept of human capital can be found even in Adam Smith's *The Wealth of Nations* (1776), way back into the 18th century:

> The second of the three portions into which the general stock of the society divides itself, is the fixed capital; of which the characteristic is, that it affords a revenue or profit without circulating or changing masters. It consists chiefly of the four following articles.
> ....
> Fourthly, of the acquired and useful abilities of all the inhabitants and member s of the society. The acquisition of such talents, by the maintenance of the acquirer during his education, study, or apprenticeship, always costs a real expense, which is a capital fixed and realized, as it were, in his person. Those talents, as they make a part of his fortune, so do they likewise that of the society to which he belongs. The improved dexterity of a workman may be considered in the same light as a machine or instrument of trade which facilitates and abridges labour, and which, though it costs a certain expense, repays that expense with a profit.
>
> (Smith, 1976, 282)

For modern economic analysis of human capital, it is Gerry Becker and Jacob Mincer, whose contributions are paramount (see Becker, 1964; Mincer, 1974). Theoretical concepts such as education as investment, rate of return to education, earnings function, on-the-job training, and general and specific training have been developed around their research in labour economics. This concept of investment in human capital is based on the premise that labour market is not a market for finished labour but for training labour, a mechanism Thurow (1975) labelled as a "job competition". This competition occurs within a firm as the employees attempt to climb up a "job ladder," and Doeringer and Piore

(1971) called it an "internal labour market." Understanding these concepts is important for proceeding to economic analysis of cooperative education. Below, these concepts are introduced together with some empirical findings in turn.

(1) Education as investment

Take a case of university education, where a high school student upon graduation is trying to decide whether to go to university or to look for a job as a high school leaver. As investment, it needs to be worthwhile, that is, the benefit of education must exceed its cost. Let Yu and Yhs be streams of annual income of a university graduate and a high school leaver respectively, where their annual income at age t are yu(t) and yhs(t). If high school is completed at age t0, university lasts for s years, and they all retire at age T (assume that they are all born on the last day of the year and they all retire on one day before the birthday), and the annual cost of education at university is cu for the s years (the educational cost is expressed as –cu in the high school leaver's income stream). Then,

$$Yu = [-cu, \dots, -cu, yu(t0 + s + 1), yu(t0 + s + 2), \dots\dots,$$
$$yu(T - 1)] \tag{3-1}$$
$$Yhs = [yh(t0 + 1), yhs(t0 + 2), \dots\dots, yhs(T - 1)] \tag{3-2}$$

For example, if one graduates high school at 18, studies at university for 4 years, and works until retirement at age 60, then

$$Yu = [-cu, -cu, -cu, -cu, yu(23), yu(24), \dots\dots, yu(59)] \tag{3-1'}$$
$$Yhs = [yhs(19), yhs(20), \dots\dots, yhs(59)] \tag{3-2'}$$

over 41 years from high school graduation to retirement. It would be reasonable to assume that one chooses to go to university if the income stream Yu is preferred to the income stream Yhs, provided that the income stream is the only difference. One way to directly compare the two streams is to evaluate the present value (PV) at time t0 + 1 defined as

$$PV(Yu) = [-cu - cu/(1 + i) - \dots - cu/(1 + i)^{(s - 1)}]$$
$$+ [yu(t0 + s + 1)/(1 + i)^s + yu(t0 + s + 2)/(1 + i)^{(s + 1)}$$
$$+ \dots.. + yu(T - 1)/(1 + i)^{(T - t0 - 2)}] \tag{3-3}$$
$$PV(Yhs) = yhs(t0 + 1) + yhs(t0 + 2)/(1 + i) + \dots\dots\dots\dots$$
$$+ yhs(T - 1)/(1 + i)^{(T - t0 - 2)} \tag{3-4}$$

where i is a discount rate. The main point of the present value calculation is that with a positive discount rate, the later the income is received, the less its value will be.
  If t0 = 18, s = 4, and T = 60, as above, then

$$PV(Yu) = [-cu - cu/(1 + i) - cu/(1 + i)^2 - cu/(1 + i)^3]$$
$$+ [yu(23)/(1 + i)^4 + yu(24)/(1 + i)^5 + \dots\dots$$
$$+ yu(59)/(1 + i)^{40}] \tag{3-3'}$$
$$PV(Yhs) = yhs(19) + yhs(20)/(1 + i) + \dots\dots + yhs(59)/(1 + i)^{40} \tag{3-4'}$$

Therefore, working as a university graduate after s years would be a better choice than working as a high school leaver now, if PV(Yu) > PV(Yhs). In descriptive terms,

    PV of university graduate's income stream (including PV
    of cost of education) >
    PV of high school leaver's income stream   (3-5)

or

    PV of income difference between university graduate and
    high school leaver from s + 1 year >
    PV of cost of education + PV of high school leaver's income
    in the first s years   (3-5)'

With the above numerical example, this would be,

    PV of income difference between university graduate
    and high school leaver from 23 to 59 >
    PV of cost of education + PV of high school leaver's
    income stream from 19 to 22   (3-5)"

Note that high school leaver's income stream from 19 to 22 is what the university graduate misses as he or she is studying or it is *opportunity cost* of going to university, while cost of education is *direct cost*. Therefore, going to university is a better choice than starting to work after leaving high school if "the present value of extra income generated by going to university over the graduate's working life exceeds the present value of the sum of its direct cost and opportunity cost." Figure 3-1 a shows a standard diagram used to explain this decision-making process. The curved lines are the *wage profiles* of a graduate and a high school leaver, both of which are upward sloping with the graduate profile starting later but higher and the high school leaver's profile starting earlier and lower, and they never cross. It needs to be emphasized that these are average wage profiles that the decision makers of educational investment would refer to, although there are many individual cases where these profiles do not represent. A box below the horizontal axis, that is B, represents the direct cost of education such as tuition fees, while A is what a high school leaver would earn when the university is studying: it is the opportunity cost of going to university. D is the income stream of a high school leaver from 22 years old to 60 years old, and C + D is the income stream of a graduate, so that C represents the stream of extra income a graduate earns over a high school leaver. Figure 3-2 converts the profiles into discounted profiles, so that the profiles become flatter as they move along age axis and the areas A, B, C, and D are transformed into *A, B, C,* and *D.*

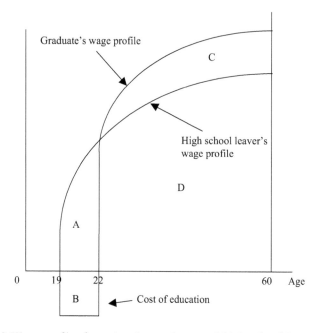

Figure 3-1 Wage profiles for university graduate and high school leaver

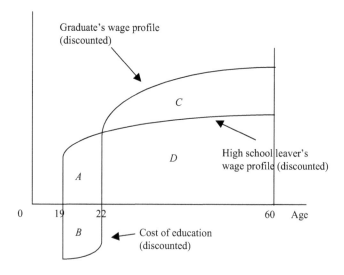

Figure 3-2 Discounted wage profiles for university graduate and high-school leaver

The decision to take the educational investment to go to university would be taken if $C > A + B$.

In this scenario, the decision depends on three things: the wage differential between a university graduate and a high school leaver, cost of education, and a discount rate. The wage differential depends on the relative supplies of and demands for university graduates and high school leavers – as the university enrolment rises and more graduates join the graduate labour market and less high school leavers join their labour market, the wage differential will be reduced. A rising high educational cost would discourage high school leavers from going to university education, or a rising living standard could make the cost of university education relatively lower to attract more students to go to university. It needs to be mentioned, however, that in many European countries, the tuition fees have been free. Finally, the discount rate reflects the value people put on future income and cost. Since the cost incurs first and the stream of income comes later, a high discount rate gives more weight to the educational cost than the income stream.

(2)   Rate of return to education, IRR, and private and social returns

The above discussion gives a theoretical explanation as to how a high school leaver would make a rational decision about his or her choice in higher education. However, it does not say much about the specific effect of this educational investment. A concept of rate of return to investment can be employed for determining the economic effect of receiving education. It is the rate at which the investment has generated its return. When the return is generated over a several periods, the rate of return becomes an *internal rate of return* (IRR), or it is the discount rate that equates the present values of cost and benefit of education in the discussion of (1). IRR is used for evaluation of monetary investment but is also appropriate here since the cost and benefit of educational investment spreads over one's lifetime. The definitions of a rate of return and IRR are given below.

Rate of return r: If cost is C0 in the first period and benefit is B1 in the second period, then

$$rC0 = B1 - C0 \text{ or } r = (B1 - C0)/C0 \tag{3-6}$$

Internal rate of return IRR: If Ct and Bt are cost and benefit in period t respectively, then over T periods of one's life since high school graduation, the following equation holds:

$$C1 + C2/(1 + IRR) + \ldots\ldots\ldots + Cs/(1 + IRR)^{(s-1)}$$
$$= B(s + 1)/(1 + IRR)^s + B(s + 2)/(1 + IRR)^{(s+1)}$$
$$+ \ldots\ldots\ldots + B(T)/(1 + IRR)^{(T-1)} \tag{3-7}$$

In this equation, in terms of educational decision to go to university as explained in (1), C's refer to the sum of direct cost and opportunity cost of education, and B's refer to the annual wage difference between a university graduate and a high school leaver.

So, if as before a graduating age for high school is 18, university course lasts for 4 years and a retirement age is 60, then IRR would be obtained by solving the following equality:

$$
\begin{aligned}
&[cu + yhs(19)] + [cu + yhs(20)]/(1 + IRR) + [cu + yhs(21)]/(1 + IRR)^2 \\
&+ [cu + yhs(22)]/(1 + IRR)^3 \\
&= [yu(23) - yhs(23)]/(1 + IRR)^4 + [yu(24) - yhs(24)]/(1 + IRR)^5 \\
&+ ..... + [yu(59) - yhs(59)]/(1 + IRR)^{40}
\end{aligned}
\tag{3-8}
$$

In fact, most of a spreadsheet software, for example, Excel has IRR function, and IRR can be derived easily by inputting the values of average annual wages for a university graduate and a high school leaver by age as well as university tuition cost.

There is a huge accumulation of data on IRR for education. Blondal et al. (2002) calculated IRR for 10 OECD (Organisation for Economic Co-operation and Development) countries. Figure 3-3 below shows some of the results – IRR for tertiary education and upper-secondary education for male and female among 10 OECD countries. Note that IRR's for upper-secondary education are calculated by comparing wages for those with upper-secondary education and those with lower-secondary education and using cost of upper-secondary education. Several points are worth noting in this international comparison. First, the most of IRRs for male and female and tertiary and upper-secondary education are higher than a typical rate of return for monetary investment. According to Ilmanen (2003), expected returns on stocks and bonds as an alternative to educational investment vary between 4 per cent and 8 per cent. Second, tertiary education seems to show

	Male		Female	
	Tertiary	Upper-secondary	Tertiary	Upper-secondary
United States	18.9	14.4	18.8	10.6
Japan	8.0	4.4	8.0	6.6
Germany	7.1	10.0	7.0	6.1
France	13.3	7.5	12.1	10.5
Italy	6.7	9.5	n.a	n.a.
United Kingdom	18.1	12.4	16.4	n.a.
Canada	8.4	11.9	10.6	10.8
Denmark	7.9	11.3	6.0	8.3
Netherlands	11.7	6.9	9.4	7.9
Sweden	9.4	3.9	7.4	n.a.
Unweighted average	11.4	9.2	10.6	8.7

Figure 3-3 IRR for 10 OECD countries (1999–2000)
Source: Blondal et al. (2002)

a higher IRR than secondary education on average, making the former a more profitable investment as a result of a large wage differential between a high school leaver and a university graduate. In fact, the differential grows by age. Third, the returns are higher for male than for female. This is probably caused by a large wage differential by sex, since the direct cost of education has no reason to differ between male and female.

So far IRR has been calculated based on the benefit and cost of education for each individual, while it is possible to define the benefit and cost of education for the society. They are called private and social IRR respectively. To the extent that education is often subsidized by the state and tax on earnings is deducted, the social cost of education would be higher than the private counterpart and social benefit of education would be higher than the private counterpart. This is supported by Blondal et al.'s (2002, 65) point:

> Since government subsidies mean that the social cost of education is higher than the private cost, social internal rates of return are generally significantly lower than the private internal rates of return. Even so, social internal rates are typically well above 5 per cent in real terms for both upper-secondary and tertiary education, suggesting that investment in education may often be a productive use of public funds.

(3)   Earnings function

There is another way to derive the rate of return to educational investment. This is due to Mincer (1974). The simple Mincerian earnings function is defined as

$$logYs = a + bS \qquad (3\text{-}9)$$

where Ys is annual earnings of a worker with s years of education and S is the years of schooling. One is to determine a and b by regressing Ys on S, by collecting individual data on annual earnings and years of education.

Mincer's more extended earnings function is defines as

$$logYst = a + bS + ct + dt^2 \qquad (3\text{-}10)$$

where Yst is annual earnings of a worker with S years of education and t years of working experience.

Mincer (1974) explains the process by which the earnings equations are derived. Instead of reproducing the full process, a simplified version is presented here (see, also, Addison and Siebert, 1979, for a compact presentation of derivation of Mincer's earnings function).

Assume one's earnings Y grows with a year of education by constant rate r and Ys is the earnings with s years of education, then the following equations hold:

$$Y1 = Y0(1 + r) \qquad (3\text{-}11)$$

$$Y2 = Y1(1 + r) = Y0(1 + r)^2 \tag{3-12}$$
$$Y3 = Y2(1 + r) = Y1(1 + r) = Y0(1 + r)^3 \tag{3-13}$$

In general,

$$Ys = Y0(1 + r)^s \tag{3-14}$$

which is equivalent to

$$\log Ys = \log Y0 + \log(1 + r)^s = \log Y0 + s \log(1 + r) \tag{3-15}$$

It is known that $\log(1 + x) \fallingdotseq x$ for a small value of x, thus

$$\log Ys = \log Y0 + Sr \tag{3-16}$$

This is the simple Mincerian earnings equation, which states that earnings Ys is related to years of education S in a log-linear form. The annual rate of return to education r is then estimated by running a regression with sample sets of observations on earnings Ys and years of education S:

$$\log Ys = a + bS \tag{3-9}$$

where estimated values of a and b signify typical earnings with no education, that is, Y0 and a rate of return to education, that is, r.

One of the problems of this simple earnings equation is the assumption that the earnings merely depend on the length of education and not on working experience – put it simply, it assumes, for example, that a 25-years-old graduate and 50-years-old graduate with differing years of experience have the same earnings. Thus, Mincer (1974) derived the extended earnings function to treat this issue as:

$$\log Yst = a + bS + ct + dt^2 \tag{3-10}$$

where t is the years of working experience and Yst is the earnings with S years of education and t years of working experience. The main point of this extension is that years of experience also adds up to the determination of earnings but at different and decreasing rate, that is, $b \neq c$ and a quadratic term dt^2 is added.

Mincer's estimation results for these equations are as below:

$$\log Ys = 7.58 + 0.070S \qquad\qquad R^2 = 0.067 \tag{3-17}$$
$$(43.8)$$
$$\log Yst = 6.20 + 0.107S + 0.081t - 0.0012t^2 \qquad R^2 = 0.285 \tag{3-18}$$
$$(72.3) \quad (75.5) \quad (-55.8)$$

(t-values in parentheses)

which shows that

(i) For the simple earnings equation, the rate of return on education is 7 per cent and the equation explains mere 6.7 per cent of the earnings determination mechanism.

(ii) For the extended earnings equation, the rate of return to education is slightly higher at 10.7 per cent and the rate of return to work experience or on-the-job training is 8.1 per cent and decreasing as work experience adds up. The explanatory power of the regression rises to 28.5 per cent.

(iii) All of these estimated coefficients are statistically significant as the absolute values of t-values are larger than 2, which means that these estimates are likely to be close to the real values.

(iv) Both rates of return to education are similar to IRR figures.
     (For an interpretation of regression result in more detail, see Chapter 7)

(4) Wage profile, on-the-job training, and general and specific training

The concept of educational investment would suggest that investment may continue into workplace by learning through working or on-the-job training (OJT). The main difference between educational investment and OJT is that in the former the whole time is spent on the investment, while in the latter, it needs to be shared between training and working. Consequently, the respective rates of return differ as in the extended Mincerian earnings equation above. The existence of OJT is interpreted as one of the reasons for a wage profile to be upward sloping. Figure 3-4 A and B show wage profiles of some of the OECD countries, where the average annual wage index (the wage of the youngest age range as 100) is measured along the vertical axis against the age on the horizontal axis for male and female by different levels of educational achievement. Three features are worth noting in these figures. First, wage profiles are generally upward sloping but decline towards the end. The upward sloping is interpreted as a result of productivity increase due to OJT based on more working experience, with an assumption that wages are based on one's productivity. A fall in wage towards the end may be caused by a decrease in productivity by age. Second, on the whole, wage profiles are higher for higher educational achievers throughout the age, which is interpreted as a result of higher level of educational investment before working life starts.

Third, female wage profiles tend to be lower than the male counterparts. The wage differential between male and female can be caused by the level of OJT. It is often observed that the female worker leaves labour force temporarily for childbirth and childcare, which can discontinue OJT for the female labour force. The male-female wage differential can be caused by sex discrimination, too.

There are two well-known theories of discrimination. One such a theory is the theory of discrimination *by taste* originally described by Becker (1957).

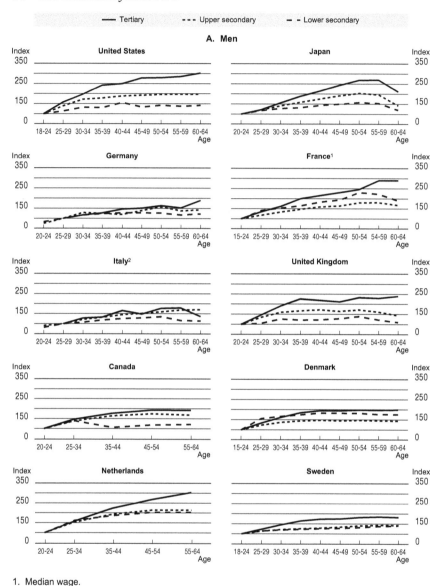

1. Median wage.
2. After tax.

Figure 3-4A Wage profiles by gender, age, and educational levels
Source: See Appendix 2.

According to Becker, whoever has a prejudice towards a certain group of employees would attach a negative value to their work, so that these workers have to be better than the rest to be accepted. The main point of his argument is that a discrimination does not stop an employer to employing a certain group of workers but makes less willing to do so. Thus, an extremely productive female worker could be employed even if the employer discriminates against them. And

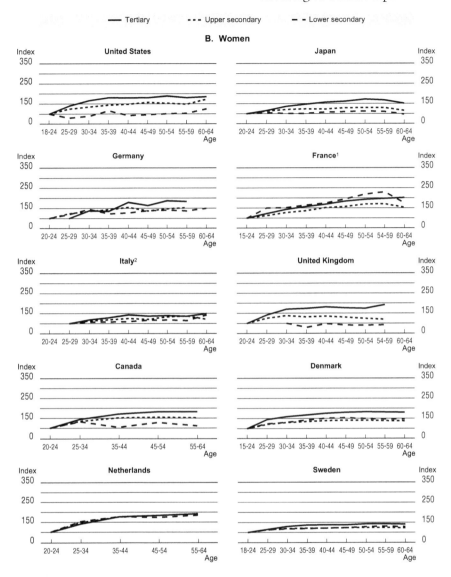

—— Tertiary   ••• Upper secondary   — — Lower secondary

1. Median wage.
2. After tax.

Figure 3-4B (Continued)

eventually, the discrimination would disappear as the discriminating employers are not employing the best labour force by leaving out the productive workers of the discriminated group and thus will be driven out of business.

The other is the theory of *statistical discrimination* originally described by Arrow (1973) and Phelps (1972). An employer may assume through the past experience, or statistical evidence, that a female employee is likely to leave the job due to childbirth and childcare, and thus suspect that OJT investment on the female employee is not going to be fully recovered. This causes the employer to reduce the investment on female and her wage could be lower as a consequence. This is true even if the female employee insists that she will not leave the job. Hence, this treatment against the female employee's wish can be considered as discrimination and yet it is a rational action from the employer's point of view. As a result, unlike the discrimination by taste, the statistical discrimination would not disappear by itself. A chapter on discrimination in labour market is provided in most of textbooks on labour economics (see, for example, Borjas, 2010), in which these two theories are explained.

Unlike educational investment, where the direct cost is covered by the student, the burden of OJT cost may fall on the employee or the employer, depending on the nature of OJT. According to Becker (1964), OJT could be either general or specific, where

> "Perfectly general" training would be equally useful in many firms and *(the productivity)* would rise by the same extent in all other firms, (p. 34) . . . *while* (c)ompletely specific training can be defined as training that has no effect on the productivity of trainees that would be useful in other firms. (p. 40)

And as examples of the two types of training, Becker (1993) referred to military training:

> The military offers training in a wide variety of skills and many are very useful in the civilian sector. . . . For example, well over 90 percent of United States commercial airplane pilots received much of their *(general)* training in the armed force. . . . (A)nd others that are only of minor use to civilians, i.e. astronauts, fighter pilots, and missile men. Such training falls within the scope of specific training because productivity is raised in the military but not much elsewhere. (pp. 39–40)

It goes without saying that the concept applies to OJT in any workplace other than the military. Generally, there is no training which is perfectly or completely general or specific. Rather, OJT has a combination of general and specific aspects with a different degree of generality/specificity. The difference in the nature of training causes a difference in the incidence of OJT, that is, who pays its cost. Generally, the more general training is, the heavier the cost burden on the employee will be and vice versa.

To see this, assume there are only two periods – the OJT period in which an employer provides OJT to an employee, and the post-OJT period in which the employee's productivity rises accordingly. Let OJT be either fully general or fully specific. If OJT is general *and* the employer pays for the training in the OJT period, the employee could move in the post-OJT period to work for other employer who offers him or her a higher wage due to the improved productivity through OJT without paying its cost. If this happened, the employer could not recuperate the OJT investment. Therefore, it would not be the employer's interest

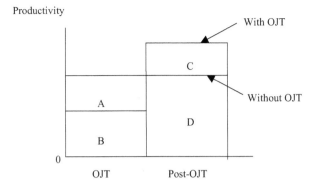

Productivity

With OJT

C

Without OJT

A

D

B

0

OJT   Post-OJT

Figure 3-5 Productivity profile of general training

to pay for the fully general training. This is illustrated in Figure 3-5, where the vertical axis measures productivity against the horizontal axis with the two periods, that is the OJT period and the post-OJT period. The horizontal line indicates the productivity without OJT, so that the productivity remains unchanged in the two periods, that is A + B in the OJT period and D in the post-OJT period. The stepped line indicates the productivity with OJT – the productivity in the OJT period is B as a result of a part of the productive activity being replaced by OJT, that is A, and C + D in the post-OJT period as a result of gaining a return on OJT investment. In fact, A is what is defined in economics as "opportunity cost" of OJT – the foregone productivity by pursuing OJT. For the sake of simplicity, it is assumed that A is the only cost of OJT. Note that A ≤ C if the OJT is to be worthwhile. If the employer pays for OJT or equivalently compensate the employee for the productivity lost for receiving OJT, the employee can receives the wage equivalent to A + B in the OJT period. In the post-OJT period, the employee could receive C + D by leaving the employer, while the employer cannot recoup the OJT cost, that is A, in the post-OJT period. In this case, the employee received OJT for free and made use of this skill elsewhere, while the employer paid for OJT but did not gain anything form it. Therefore, for employers, it is not worth paying for general training, while it is so for employees.

Now assume, instead, OJT is specific and the employee pays for the training in the OJT period. The employee would face a risk of not raising productivity in the post-OJT period, if the employment is discontinued with the present employer. Therefore, it would not be the employee's interest to pay for the training if it is specific. What about the employer? The employer would be willing to pay for the OJT, as the employee is likely to stay on hoping that some of the increased productivity may give him or her a rise in wage. To describe it visually, consider Figure 3-5 again. If the employer pays fully for the specific training by compensating the worker for the foregone productivit due to OJT, the employee receives A + B though his or her the productivity is merely B. The employee will be indifferent between remaining with the present employer and moving elsewhere, as he or she would expect to receive D in both cases – the present employer will take the return on OJT,

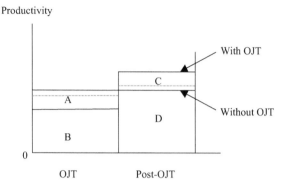

Figure 3-6 Productivity profile of firm-specific training productivity

that is C, and a new employer will pay wage without OJT since the OJT he or she has received does not raise productivity above D elsewhere. In this case, it would be the present employer's interest to keep the employee, since the OJT investment cannot be recouped if the employee moves. This makes the employer pay slightly higher wage in the post-OJT period, to give the employee an incentive to stay on. This is illustrated in Figure 3-6, with the employee receiving a wage slightly below A + B in the OJT period and a wage slightly above D in the post-OJT period as indicated by a dotted stepped line.

In reality, any OJT is likely to have elements of both general and specific training. As a result, the cost of OJT is likely to be shared by the employer and the employee.

(5)   Educational credential as a signal

There is another theory in economics to explain why education can raise one's earnings. According to Spence (1973), a completion of schooling is a proof of one's ability and it could be used as a signal for his or her productivity and thus earnings at work. His model is based on two basic assumptions. First, people are born with different levels of innate ability, which are positively related to their academic performance at school as well as productivity at work. Second, the ability is not known to others. With a simplified numerical example, Spence (1973) showed that even if schooling does not raise one's productivity, as argued in the human capital theory, the school credential can earn him or her a higher wage by acting as a signal for his or her higher productivity at work.

A simple example based on the Spence's (1973) concept of the signalling mechanism is presented here. Suppose that there are 100 university students, with 50 of them having higher ability H and the rest with lower ability L and the student ability affects academic performance at study as well as productivity at work. The difference in academic performance is reflected in the cost of completing university degree (CE) such that $CE_H = 2$ and $CE_L = 6$, or it costs less to the students with high ability, while the more able students have higher productivity

Table 3-1 A simple numerical example for signalling

Group	Population	Productivity = Wage (P)	Cost of education at university (CE)
H	50	$P_H = 10$	$CE_H = 2$
L	50	$P_L = 5$	$CE_L = 6$
Total	100	$P = 7.5$	

at work (P) than the less able students such that $P_H = 10$ and $P_L = 5$. They would be paid according to their productivity provided that the employer can distinguish the two groups. Otherwise, everyone will be paid the average productivity, that is, 7.5. Table 3-1 summarizes the example.

As it was assumed, however, the employer cannot identify the ability of the students. Instead, consider that students are offered the wages based on educational achievement, that is, a wage is 10 with university degree and 5 otherwise. Assume further that students decide whether or not to obtain university degree based on the future earnings net of cost of education, that is P – CE. The students with ability H find it worthwhile obtaining the university degree, as his or her net earnings with the degree, that is $P_H - CE_H = 10 - 2 = 8$, is greater than the earnings without it, that is $P_L = 5$, while the students with ability L find it otherwise, as his or her net earnings with the degree, that is $P_H - CE_L = 10 - 6 = 4$, is smaller than the earnings without it, that is $P_L = 5$. When this occurs, the students manage to "self-select" themselves based on the combination of cost of education and wage differentials.

It is easy to see the result depends on the relative values attached to the productivity and cost of education. For example, if, instead, $CE_L = 4$, an easy calculation can show that both H and L students would decide to obtain the degree $(P_H - CE_L = 10 - 4 = 6 > P_L = 5)$. However, it would mean the low ability students are paid more than their productivity (remember that the assumption is that completing university degree does not raise the productivity of the low ability students), which is no financially sustainable for the employer. In the end, the only sustainable case with a uniform wage is the case where everyone is paid the average productivity, that is 7.5. In the signalling literature, the former is called a *separating equilibrium* and the latter the *pooling equilibrium*. The intuitive explanation is that if an educational credential is to be an effective signalling device, it should be worthwhile for some group but not for others to separate the groups.

Note also that the positive relationship between wage and educational credential holds for both the signalling model and the human capital model. It implies that even if an empirical result proves the positive relationship, one cannot conclude if this is due to education's role as signalling or human capital accumulation. There are empirical studies to verify the education's signalling role. Riley (1979) divided workers into jobs where productivity is more observable and less observable to see validity of the signalling hypothesis. Based on American data from the Current Population Survey, his result indicated that educational qualification was less important for the former, supporting the hypothesis. Wolpin (1977) compared self-employed and employees in a private sector, using the National Bureau of Economic Research-Thorndike sample. If education acts as a signal of one's productivity, it would be more useful when one is employed than self-employed. His analysis showed that to attain a given earnings level, the employees needed higher educational level than self-employed, supporting the signalling hypothesis.

Other empirical studies compared the human capital aspect and signalling aspect of education. As pointed out earlier, a positive relationship between an educational level and earnings holds for both the human capital hypothesis and the signalling hypothesis, not sufficient to support one or the other. Kroch and Sjoblom (1994) used "years of schooling" and "rank of schooling" in the earnings equation to distinguish the effect of education in American data from the Current Population Survey-Social Security Administration-Internal Revenue Service Extract Match File and Michigan Panel Study on Income Dynamics. Rank of schooling is a variable to rank a given level of education within the distribution of educational attainment in a given year. For example, as the general educational level rises, a rank of high school graduation would fall over the years. Their finding was that the value of schooling is in the human capital accumulation rather than signalling. Bedard (2001) compared the reaction of high school dropouts, high school graduates, and university enrolees when entering university becomes easier, using American data from the National Longitudinal Survey for Young Men and Young Women in 1966 and 1968. If education acts as a signal, it is argued, easier access to university would send more students from the high school graduate pool lowering the general academic level of the high school graduate pool. This would generate less incentive to obtain high school graduation as a signal causing more dropouts. If on the contrary, education acts as human capital accumulation, easier access to university would raise a high school graduation rate as well as a university enrolment rate. The empirical analysis concluded that the dropouts are higher with easier access to university, supporting signalling hypothesis.

(6)   Other factors determining educational attainment and socioeconomic outcome

So far the causal relationship between education and earnings or income have been discussed. However, in real life many other factors are responsible for determining both educational decision and earnings. Figure 3-7 attempts to simplify this rather complex interactive relationships among these factors. The factors are grouped into four groups – genetic element, environmental element, which is subdivided into family background and socioeconomic background, reinforcement, and socioeconomic outcome. The reinforcement, that is educational or OJT decision, which was discussed earlier as human capital and signalling, could be affected by one's personal traits by birth such as cognitive and non-cognitive skills, sex and race (Arrow A), although the way sex and race

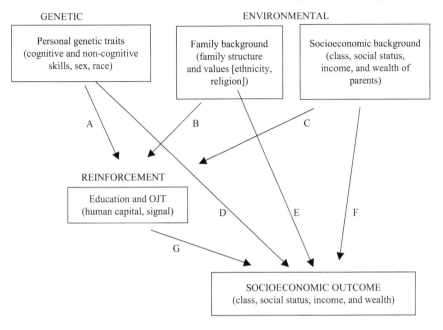

GENETIC   ENVIRONMENTAL

Personal genetic traits
(cognitive and non-cognitive
skills, sex, race)

Family background
(family structure
and values [ethnicity,
religion])

Socioeconomic background
(class, social status,
income, and wealth of
parents)

A   B   C

REINFORCEMENT

Education and OJT
(human capital, signal)

D   E   F

G

SOCIOECONOMIC OUTCOME
(class, social status, income, and wealth)

Figure 3-7 The interactions of factors affecting individual socioeconomic outcome

influence the educational decision may be more environmental than genetic. The environmental background that affects the reinforcement decision may be categorized into family background such as family structure and size and family values, for example ethnicity and religion (Arrow B), and socioeconomic background such as class, social status, income, and wealth of parents (Arrow C). Socioeconomic outcome, which can be expressed in terms of achieved class, social status, income or wealth could be affected by one's personal traits (Arrow D), family background (Arrow E), and socioeconomic background of the parents (Arrow F) as well as reinforcement (Arrow G).

Verifying some of these arrows has been a subject of empirical investigations. Bowles et al. (2005) offer a collection of research articles to determine factors influencing one's economic success using mostly American data. While there is a huge literature on how genetic and environmental factors bring about one's socioeconomic success particularly in the fields of psychology and sociology, this chapter concentrates on results which are relevant to the present discussion from Bowles et al. (2005) as well other related research in this field.

The focus of socioeconomic factors will be on quantifiable measures such as income and wealth as opposed to qualitative measures such as social class and status. The correlation between economic status of parent and son was generally found to be low in the United States in the earlier research. For example, in the survey article of Becker and Tomes (1986), the average of parent's and son's income elasticity was mere 0.15 – a higher income of a parent would raise the son's income by mere 15 per cent (Arrow F). However, more recent research such as Mazumder (2005) has pointed out that the weak correlation was due to measurement error, and when the error was corrected, the correlation appeared to be as much as three time of what Becker and Tomes (1986) found (Arrow F). Hertz (2005) found that the income correlation between parent and child is particularly strong at the top and the bottom of the income distribution, that is wealth and poverty, transmit intergenerationally. Intergenerational transmission elasticities are calculated for consumption, wealth, and years of schooling to be 0.68, 0.50, 0.29 respectively as opposed to income and earnings elasticities of 0.43 and 0.34 in Mulligan (1997), which shows that consumption and wealth accumulation patterns are transmitted more strongly (Arrows E and F). Osborne (2005) offered an extended human capital model to include father's earnings and personality as non-cognitive skills, son's IQ and personality, that is non-cognitive skills, as well as years of schooling and working, as determining factors of son's earnings and pointed out the importance of the non-cognitive personality traits (Arrows D, G, and F). Hertz (2005) pointed out the inheritance of wealth and income-enhancing group memberships such as race to cause the intergenerational transmission of income, which explains that race affects the transmission not as a genetic factor but as a socioeconomic factor (Arrow D or F).

The role of genetic inheritance of intelligence has been studied by various groups. Bouchard and McGue (1981) surveyed over 100 studies on familial resemblance in measured intelligence and found that the correlation of IQ between parents and offspring to range from 0.42 to 0.72, indicating the genetic factor to play a considerable role. On the non-cognitive personality traits, Loehlin (2005) considered five elements: extraversion, agreeableness, conscientiousness, neuroticism, and openness, and found their transmission from parents to child not to be significant. Duncan et al. (2005) investigated whether there are intergenerational transmissions of family values such as parenting style, home environment, and role modelling alongside genetic traits and socioeconomic status. Their result shows that what is passed down the generations is a set of specific rather than general competencies.

A series of studies on twins were conducted to differentiate the effects of genetic and environmental factors on earnings (Arrows D, E, and F). One of the pioneering works of economic analysis in this area is Taubman (1976). He collected and compared a sample consisting of monozygotic, or identical, twins and dizygotic, or fraternal, twins, where the former have all their genes in common and the latter share roughly half of their genes. The idea is to separate the effects of genetic and family influences on earnings. He concludes that "it would seem that much of the inter- and intragenerational inequality of earnings is related to who one's parents are." Bjorklund et al. (2005) used Swedish twin data to conclude the earnings variation is derived more from environmental rather than genetic factors. Bowles et al. (2001) in their meta-analysis of over 20 studies shows that the effect of cognitive score on earnings is small and less than that of years of schooling (Arrows A, D, and G). Smith (1999)'s argument about "Healthy Bodies and Thick Wallets" based on data from the Panel Study of Income Dynamics seems to explain how family values can affect socioeconomic outcome (Arrow E). Wealth appears to be one of the major factors for determining the socioeconomic success. However, Mulligan (1997) points out that the proportion of wealth subject to inheritance tax was as small as 2 to 4 per cent in the United States during 1960 and 1995, implying that the extent of transmission of wealth is not substantial, while Bowles et al. (2005) too suggest that the parent-child wealth transmission may not be significant based on the Panel Study of Income Dynamics data (Arrow F).

It would be reasonable to conclude that intergenerational transmission of income or earnings do exist, but its mechanism is rather complex except to say that cognitive trait does not seem to play a significant role, while education does. Swift (2005) and Feldman et al. (2005) question whether intergenerational transmission of environmental factors are fair. It is difficult to disallow parental self-interest and altruism for the future benefit of their children for the sake of social equality and justice.

4 An economic analysis of cooperative education

This chapter analyses cooperative education based on the theoretical frameworks presented in Chapter 3. As cooperative education involves academic study and work experience, it has elements of educational human capital investment at university as well as on-the-job training (OJT) at workplace. Thus, these elements are discussed in turn. To do so, cooperative education is defined as consisting of *university study* period and *work experience* period, where the former is divided into two periods to "sandwich" the latter as in the British "sandwich programme" described in Chapter 2, so that the whole cooperative education consists of three periods – pre-work experience university study period, work experience period, and post-work experience university study period. Also, the coop students are assumed to be remunerated during the work experience. This is a simplified form of cooperative education programme, as there are many variations particularly about the number and length of work experience periods. This form, however, should be able to represent the fundamental features of cooperative education, that is, an interaction between study and work or equivalently, university and workplace.

(1) Cooperative education as human capital investment

Cooperative education may be considered as one of variations within a framework of human capital investment. To illustrate the case, consider a simple example. Let university's academic degree last for 4 years and a cooperative education programme offers a year of work experience at the end of third year, so that the coop student would come back to complete the degree after the work experience by staying 1 more year at university, which makes university career to be 5 years instead of 4 years with an orthodox academic degree. Based on the discussion earlier on present value of lifetime earnings net of educational cost for university graduates and high school leavers, university graduates with and without cooperative education will have their present value, PV_{UCE} and PV_U respectively as below.

$$PV_{UCE} = -C - C/(1 + r) - C/(1 + r)^2 + Y_{CE}/(1 + r)^3 - C/(1 + r)^4 \\ + Y_{UCE24}/(1 + r)^5 + \ldots \qquad (4\text{-}1)$$

$$PV_U = -C - C/(1+r) - C/(1+r)^2 - C/(1+r)^3 + Y_{U23}/(1+r)^4$$
$$+ Y_{U24}/(1+r)^5 + \ldots \tag{4-2}$$

where C is the annual cost of education, which is assumed to be unchanged over the degree programme, Y_{CE} is the annual remuneration or earnings of coop student during work experience, Y_{CEt} is the annual earnings of an graduate with cooperative education at age t, and Y_{Ut} is the annual earnings of an graduate without cooperative education at age t counting the university entry age as 19, and r is a discount rate. In actual cases, some cooperative programmes charge the registration fees, and here such cost is included in Y_{CE}, that is, Y_{CE} is the coop earnings net of the coop fee. The difference in the income stream of a coop student and a non-coop student appears in the fourth and fifth years, that is, cooperative education generates coop earnings during work experience in the fourth year, but there is a year delay for starting the stream of earnings from employment.

If cooperative education is to have economic merit over orthodox university degree programme, then the present value of the wage premium for cooperative education over the working periods needs to be greater than the net cost of cooperative education that appeared in the third and fourth years over the academic programme. That is,

$$PV_{UCE} > PV_U$$
$$\text{or } (Y_{UCE24} - Y_{U24})/(1+r)^5 + (Y_{UCE25} - Y_{U25})/(1+r)^6 + \ldots$$
$$+ (Y_{UCEt} - Y_{Ut})/(1+r)^{T-1} >$$
$$(Y_{U23} + C)/(1+r)^4 - (Y_{CE} + C)/(1+r)^3 \tag{4-3}$$

It is easier to grasp what is going on by letting r = 0. Then, the inequality becomes,

$$(Y_{UCE24} - Y_{U24}) + (Y_{UCE25} - Y_{U25}) + \ldots + (Y_{UCE59} - Y_{U59}) > Y_{U23} - Y_{CE} \tag{4-4}$$

In another words, cooperative education is worthwhile if the sum of the stream of cooperative education wage premium, that is $Y_{UCEt} - Y_{Ut}$, exceeds the difference between the first year earinings of a non-coop graduate, that is Y_{U23}, and that of coop student during work experience Y_{CE}. Introducing non-zero discount rate would alter the condition but not greatly as r is not a large value, that is, typically a one digit figure in percentage terms. Certainly, what cooperative education needs to add up over an orthodox university education programme is far below what was needed for university education over high school certificate, as the direct and opportunity costs of cooperative education is much lower. In any case, cooperative education needs to make the graduate more productive than the orthodox university programme.

This depends on whether the coop students can effectively use the work experience for the final and fifth year's study.

Internal Rate of Return (IRR) may be calculated for cooperative education, where the alternative is without cooperative education, so that IRR should satisfy $PV_{UCE} = PV_U$, or

$$
(Y_{UCE24} - Y_{U24})/(1 + r)^5 + (Y_{UCE25} - Y_{U25})/(1 + r)^6 +
$$
$$
\dots + (Y_{UCE59} - Y_{U59})/(1 + r)^{40} = (Y_{U23} + C)/(1 + r)^4
$$
$$
- [Y_{CE} - C/(1 + r)^3] \qquad (4\text{-}5)
$$

It would be an interesting empirical application of the concept of IRR. It would also have a useful implications particularly for policy makers, as it can quantify the effect of cooperative education. Unfortunately, no extensive data are available yet – all one needs is to ask whether cooperative education was undertaken when collecting individual data on earnings.

(2)   Cooperative education as on-the job training

In economics and in labour economics literature in particular, OJT is also refereed as "learning-by-doing." It is a learning process at workplace and in that sense work experience in cooperative education is no different, except that the result of cooperative education is first reflected at university in the post-work experience period. Consequently, the earlier discussion on OJT applies to work experience in cooperative education. OJT was categorized into general and (firm-)specific, where the former is training of skills that is equally useful and thus raises productivity to the same extent in all firms, while the latter is training of skills that is useful and thus raises productivity only in the firm where it was acquired. One would expect work experience to be general rather than specific in nature, as coop students are not necessarily considering of committing themselves to the coop firm when they graduate.

In cooperative education literature, on the other hand, it is more common to talk in terms of soft (or generic or social) skills and hard (or cognitive or technical) skills. Soft skills refer to all-purpose skills that form the basis for a wide range of tasks and occupations, which include communication skills, motivation, team work, problem solving, positive attitude to work, while hard skills refer to specific skills required for a particular occupations (see, for example, Brimble et al., 2011, and Marini, 1998).

So what is the difference between the general and firm-specific skill dichotomy of OJT in labour economics and the soft and hard skill dichotomy of work experience in cooperative education? The main difference is that the general and firm-specific argument concentrates on firm-specificity, while the soft and hard skill argument concentrates on the occupation-specificity. While most of soft skills are general skills, not all hard skills are firm specific but "occupation specific" – for example, some engineering skills are required for engineering occupation but can be used in more than on a specific engineering firm. The comparison of these concepts is shown in Table 4-1.

Table 4-1 Skill specificity

Degree of Specificity	All-purpose	Occupation specific	Firm specific
OJT	General training (or General skills)		Specific training (or Firm-specific skills)
Cooperative Education	Soft skills	Hard skills	

So what does a coop student learn during work experience? And who pays for the work experience? Answering these questions requires first determining whether coop students learn soft skills or hard skills and then analysing the incidence within the OJT theoretical framework. There has been a long tradition of cooperative education in the field of engineering since Schneider and cooperative education seems to best fit to prepare these students with the hard skills for workplace. What one typically finds in the actual case studies for cooperative education programmes (see, for example, research papers in annual World Association for Cooperative Education [WACE] conferences) is that "work experience prepares these students to best make use of their hard skills by acquiring soft skills" through the combination of the two. Today, cooperative education is no longer confined to science and engineering disciplines. For other disciplines such as social sciences and humanities, the students seem to require soft skills even more, as many of them would seek employment in the service sector. Therefore most of the skill training during work experience may be considered to be soft skills or general skills.

So who pays for the work experience? In most of cases, the remuneration for a coop student is set at a level somewhat below that of a newly employed graduate on full-time contract. This wage gap can be caused by two reasons. One is the difference in productivity due to a different length of education – in our example, the coop student has completed 3 years and still has a year to complete the degree after a completion of the work experience, while a non-coop graduate has completed the full 4 years when the employment starts. Another is due to paying of training cost. The wage may be lower as the coop student "pays" for receiving training of the soft skills – as it was explained earlier, in principle the cost of general training is paid not by a firm but by a worker, as there is no guarantee that the coop student will return to the coop firm upon graduation and the firm recuperate the OJT investment. A newly employed graduate does receive general training but may not always pay the cost fully as he or she is likely to stay longer at the firm than a coop student on work experience, allowing the firm to have more time to recover the cost. This generates a well-known two distinctive curves for a wage profile and productivity in labour economics, in which an employee is initially paid more than his or her productivity, but the productivity eventually overtake the wage profile

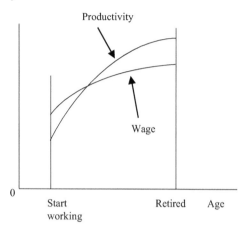

Figure 4-1 Wage and productivity profiles

(see Figure 4-1). In sum, a coop student receives OJT of general skills during work experience with earnings somewhat below non-coop graduate earnings.

(3) Cooperative education as a signal

In the simplified model of signalling based on Spence (1973) in Chapter 3, the existence of educational credential as a signal depended crucially on the positive relationship between one's academic ability at school and productivity at work, so that higher earnings is related to lower cost of education. In reality, however, one's productive ability is multifaceted and an academic credential may not be the sole signal for one's productive ability or even worse academic performance and workplace productivity may not be closely related. When this link between productivity and academic ability becomes weak or breaks down, observation at work experience would be a better signal than the academic credential. It is still a signal because work experience and actually work are not identical and the coop student will not necessary return to the coop firm after graduation. Yet it is likely to be a more accurate signal for two reasons – first the task itself is work related, and second, it is observed and evaluated by employers as well as academics.

(4) A case study: cooperative education and socioeconomic climate in Japan

It has been shown that cooperative education can play an important role in connecting study and work through building soft skills for coop students to prepare them for employment. It can also act as a signal to firms for the potential productivity of the coop student. It is important to point out that cooperative education is not to substitute but to complement orthodox education and OJT – in most of universities, cooperative education constitutes a part of undergraduate programme, where the main part is still the orthodox education. A similar argument applies to firms and OJT. Cooperative education needs to be a part of firm's OJT process, as OJT, or learning-by-doing, is an ongoing process that never stops as long as one is in employment. Yet, the importance of cooperative education varies with socioeconomic background of a country and its era. For example, its popularity in the post-war USA grew with the demand for skilled workers of new technology, as explained in Chapter 2. It also depend on the effectiveness of orthodox education and OJT, as it complements them.

A good illustrative example of how cooperative education could play its role in economy is Japan in recent years. Among the developed economies, Japan has been lagging behind in development of cooperative education. It was as late as in 1999 that the Ministry of Education (MEXT) officially used the term *career education,* the Japanese equivalent of cooperative education. Tradition-ally, Japanese firms are said to offer "lifetime employment" and "seniority wage." to the employees. The former refers to a long-term employment relationship where an employee is loyal to the firm until the retirement and the latter refers to a system where a wage rises with years of service to a particular firm making changing an employer often a cause of a wage drop. This system allows firms to provide an extensive and long term OJT, often taking over the skill building role of universities. This weakens the connection between university education and acquiring of hard skills, almost reducing the role of the Japanese universities to providers of signals for potential productivity rather than of specific skills and knowledge. In short, a division of labour exists between universities and firms in which the former sort out the students by ability and the latter recruit stu-dents with high potentials to train the with OJT.

This system was becoming unsustainable for two reasons towards the end of 20th century. One of them is the collapse of bubble economy of late 1980s and over a decade of recession known as the "lost decade." This has made the extensive and long-term investment in human capital not worthwhile. Japanese firms started to shift from training unexperienced graduates towards employing experienced workers during this period. Labour Force Survey shows, for example, that among young male and female employees between age 25 and 34, the proportion of non-full time employees has risen from 10.7 per cent in 1988 to 26 per cent in 2012, suggesting firms are not providing as much OJT as before (see Figure 4-2). Japanese universities are looking into filling this gap by providing cooperative education alongside MEXT policy to encourage the study and work connection.

The other is the demographic change of university entrants. With a decreasing youth population and a number of places available at university unchanged, the enrolment rate has been rising. According to MEXT's School Basic Survey, the enrolment rate, which is the number of entrants divided by the total population of the age group, for universities and colleges of male and female high school leavers rose from 36.3 per cent in 1990 to 56.2 per cent in 2012, while the population of 18 years old fell from about 2 million to 1.2 million during this

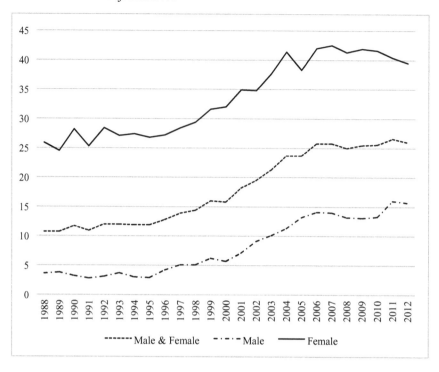

Figure 4-2 The trend in per cent of non-full time employees (1988–2012)

Source: Ministry of International Affairs and Communications, Labour Force Survey, Japan Annual report 1988-2012

period (See Table 4-2). Furthermore, 2007 marked a year when the number of high school leavers who intend to study at university has fallen to equate the number of university places for the first time. These facts suggest that the competition to enter university has become less intense with a possibility of educational credential not functioning as a signal, thereby making cooperative education as a better signal.

MEXT published "a report on internship practices at higher education institutions" in 2011 (MEXT, 2013), which describes the present situation on study and work programme in Japan. The percentage of higher education institutions offering internship programme was 23.7 per cent in 1998 and rose to 70.5 per cent in 2011, while the percentage of student participating in the programme was 0.6 per cent in 1998 and rose to 2.2 per cent in 2011. As for the length of work experience, 63.1 per cent of them lasted less than 2 weeks in 2007 and there was a slight reduction to 61.6 per cent in 2011, while 7.6 per cent of work experience lasted over a month in 2007, and there was an increase to 11.5 per cent in 2011. But a remuneration for work experience was not found to be a common practice, which is understandable considering its short period. Despite the needs for cooperative education to play an active role in economy, the reality has not caught up with the expectation – its popularity is rising, but a faster movement may be encouraged.

Part III

The empirical assessment: a statistical/econometric evaluation of cooperative education

5 Statistical/econometric tools to analyse the effectiveness of cooperative education

The theoretical analysis of cooperative education has been dealt with extensively in the disciplines other than economics particularly in psychology and education, where concepts such as Kolb's experiential learning (Kolb, 1984), Dewey's learning model (Dewey, 1916), Lewin's action research (Lewin, 1946), and Piaget's learning and cognitive development (Piaget, 1985) appear, as has been briefly introduced in Chapter 2. Such theories can suggest mechanisms by which cooperative education brings about its effects on academic performance and on employment outcome. However, one may need to know *to what extent* it works as much as *how* it works. This has a practical implication. Often the outcome of educational input requires a long time to materialize. This makes it difficult to pinpoint the causal relationship, and cooperative education is no exception. The practitioners of cooperative education are well aware of the labour-intensive nature of the programme, which can cause a considerable financial burden to whoever runs it. In order to convince the bearer of the programme, be it the university administration, the government, or students, that such a programme is worthwhile, it needs to prove its cost-effectiveness. Following the human capital theory introduced in Chapters 3 and 4, one may show that the present value of lifetime wage profile differentials between a coop graduate and non-coop graduate more than offsets the cost of cooperative education. If this holds, then the cooperative programme can show its raison d'être, particularly to the university administration to support it, the government to fund it, and potential students to undertake it. However, the existing data on wages may not have information on coop experience alongside age, gender, years of working experience, and educational level.

But there are other ways to evaluate the effectiveness. In the following chapters, the effectiveness of cooperative education on student's academic performance, employment placement outcome, and job performance are considered in turn. But before doing so, this chapter provides first some discussions about what factors or variables are used and how they are analysed. This will be followed by a brief survey on statistical studies of the effectiveness of cooperative education.

(1)   Interactive mechanism and its factors around cooperative education

Fig. 3-6 illustrated the interactive mechanism of factors that influences one's socio-economic development. This is the starting point of the statistical analysis but some modifications are necessary to apply this framework to the analysis of cooperative education. Fig. 5-1 is the modified and simplified version for cooperative education, where *pre-university background* replaces *genetic* and *environmental, reinforcement* is divided into I and II, and *socioeconomic outcome* is replaced by *economic outcome.* This type of diagram is sometimes called a *path diagram,* and a theoretical framework based on this concept is known as *path analysis.* Path analysis is both a concept and a statistical tool to determine causal relationships among variables within a given structure. The concept is useful for disentangling causal relationships among the variables (see, for example, Lleras (2005) and Tunali (1987)).

Path analysis was first introduced by Sewall Wright, a geneticist, who sought to disentangle genetic influences across generations (Wright, 1921). Wright's contribution to investigations in social science went further, when he subsequently wrote an article on an analysis of corn market, where he applied his approach to economic analysis of supply-and-demand interaction (Wright, 1925), and an article on an identification problem of simultaneous equation system, where he discussed how to identify supply and demand from given data (Wright, 1934). It is worth

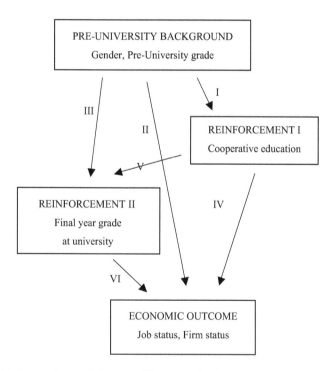

Figure 5-1 Interactions of factors affecting individual academic and employment outcome

noting that his interests in simultaneity and identification appeared long before they started to be treated as a standard concept in econometrics.

It was later introduced in 1960s to sociologists for investigations in processes involved in status attainment. In econometrics, it is better known as a "recursive system" of a "simultaneous equation model" (also sometimes called a "structural equation model"): see Blalock (1985), Kaplan (2000), and Maruyama (1997) for social science at large and Goldberger (1972) for economcs, while most of textbooks in econometrics such as Greene (2008) and Wooldridge (2009, 2010) have a chapter on a simultaneous equation model.

The quantitative investigations to follw need to answer the following questions – (i) what influences the decision to undertake cooperative education programme, (ii) does cooperative education have an effect on academic performance, and (iii) does cooperative education have an effect on employment outcome. For each of these questions, factors or variables to investigate these relationships need to be identified.

(i)   What influences the decision to undertake cooperative education programme?

This question relates to Arrow I. As will be discussed in the brief survey, many researchers suspect that undertaking cooperative education is not a random decision – smarter students tend to undertake the programme, in which case its success could be overestimated. In order to use quantifiable data, gender and pre-university grade are used, where the former is a dummy variable, that is, 1 if male and 0 if female, and the latter is a cardinal value which express the student academic marks at high school such as a national examination result. Where such a national measure is not available, the exam result in the first year may be used – throughout the empirical analysis of the book, Grade Point Average (GPA) in the first year is used as a proxy to one's high school academic achievement. Cooperative education can be a dummy variable, that is, 1 if undertaken and 0 otherwise. Or it could be a quantity variable such as a number of cooperative education related subjects undertaken, or a length or a number of work experience. Note that the dummy variable cannot be used if it is mandatory as in some institutions.

(ii)   Does cooperative education have an effect on academic performance?

This question relates to Arrows II and III. The pre-university background variables such as gender and pre-university grade as well as the reinforcement I variable such as cooperative education can be used to check their influence on the reinforcement II variable such as the final year grade at university. It is important to separate and clarify the causal relationship between cooperative education and the academic grade. In particular, the use of overall grade may be avoided as it may include grades obtained before cooperative education was undertaken, since this could reverse the causal relationship. In a similar manner, although it is not explicitly discussed in the book, the effect of cooperative education on student's attitude towards studying can be investigated. A multiple choice question, say, from 0 with "strongly disagree" to 5 with "strongly agree," to ask the effect of cooperative education towards one's attitudes towards academic study may be used to see whether cooperative education motivates students to pursue academic career at university.

(iii)   *Does cooperative education have an effect on employment outcome?*

This question relates to Arrows II and IV and VI. The effect of cooperative education on employment outcome may be investigated in several ways. The following two approaches are taken in this book. First is the quality of job placement after graduation, where the quality may be expressed by the status of firm, for example listed or not listed, or by the description of job, for example full-time or part-time. Thus, the investigation is made to see whether such outcomes are influenced by the cooperative education experience together with gender, pre-university grade, and final year grade. Second is the attitude towards job. Employees may be asked whether their present attitudes are influenced by their cooperative education experience though multiple choice answer from strongly agree to strongly disagree as above. Based on Human Capital Theory as explained in earlier chapter, perhaps what is most required is the evidence that cooperative education raises one's earnings. A comparison of wages of coop graduate and non-coop graduates would be needed for such an investigation – or the lifetime earnings of these two groups to be precise. Several difficulties have to be overcome. First, the sample graduates have to be traced by mail or otherwise, who are no longer at university, unlike the investigations of (i) and (ii). Second, it is difficult to obtain data on earnings that also contain cooperative education data – one may have to start such a data set. Finally, a longitudinal data that extend through one's student's life and working life would be ideal. In all, more systematic and continuous data collection is called for.

(2)   Statistical/econometric tools

In the following chapters, several quantitative methods will be employed to answer these questions. These methods can be categorized into two groups – a statistical testing and a multiple regression analysis. The statistical testing is based on a normal distribution of samples, and t tests, z tests, χ^2 tests, and F tests may be applied depending on what needs to be tested. An F test used in this context is better known as an analysis of variance (ANOVA). A z test may be used to compare proportions in two groups – for example, the male/female ratios for coop and non-coop student groups. Generally, if two or more groups are compared – for example, the male/female ratios for three student groups of a type I coop, a type II coop and non-coop, χ^2 test is used instead. This implies that a binary comparison may be conducted by both methods, that is a z test and a χ^2 test – it is rather confusing that some researchers use the former and others use the latter. A t test may be used to compare average values in two groups – for example, the average exam marks for coop and non-coop student groups. Generally, if two or more groups are compared – for example, the average exam marks for, say, three student groups of a type I coop, a type II coop and a non-coop, ANOVA is used instead. This implies that a binary comparison may be conducted by both methods, that is a t test and ANOVA – here again, it is rather confusing that some researchers use the former and others use the latter. In the numerical examples to follow, these equivalences, that is of a z test and a χ^2 test, and a t test and an F test will be verified.

One suspects, however, that the different outcome for coop and non-coop groups may rise for other attributes hidden in these two groups – for example, coop students may perform better academically not because cooperative education has a positive effect on academic study but academically competent students tend to follow cooperative education programme in the first place. A concept of a path analysis can be used as explained based on a multiple regression analysis, in which the causal effects of "independent (or exogenous) variables" on "dependent (or endogenous) variable" are estimated for relevant relationships. It can identify effects of each independent variables on the dependent variable separately. In this book, this approach is referred to as an *econometric* as opposed to *statistical* approach.

Two issues need to be clarified for a regression analysis of the econometric approach. One is the functional form of the causal relationship. It is customary to assume a linear relationship as it is the simplest form to express a causal relationship. However, when the dependent variable takes non-continuous variables such as one/zero binary values, a use of non-linear relationship such as logistic or accumulative normal distribution curve is theoretically more appropriate. The functional form for estimation then is usually one of linear, logit, and probit. Among the three, the linear model is the simplest and intuitive, while the other two have more theoretical rigour. When the choice is multiple rather than binary as in ranking a level of satisfaction, say from 0 to 5, the choice model can be extended to an ordered logit model or an ordered probit model. The other issue is the estimation method. Most commonly used procedures are a least square method and a maximum likelihood method. Calculation process is much simpler for the former, and a simple spreadsheet programme such as Excel can handle it given that the data set is not too large, while the latter needs a higher-powered software programmes such as EVIEWS and SPSS, although it can cope with more complicated functions – in fact, logit models and probit models cannot be estimated with a least square method on Excel sheet but need a maximum likelihood estimation found in a higher-powered software than Excel. In the following chapters, the main estimation tool is the least square method as its concept and the resultant estimates are intuitively easier to follow than the maximum likelihood method, although a comparison with logit and probit models is made wherever appropriate.

(3) Past studies on statistical/econometric analysis of the effectiveness of cooperative education

There have been several different quantitative analysis to verify the effectiveness of cooperative education programmes. This section briefly introduces some of the past investigations with emphases on the sample characteristics, method used, and the result derived. The analyses can be divided into three types in terms of the method used – a direct comparison, a statistical testing, and a regression analysis.

Examples of a direct comparison are Hartley and Smith (2000), Zegwaard and McCurdy (2008), and Mendez (2008). Hartley and Smith (2000) asked 57 students of management courses in an American university in 1988 about the effectiveness of their cooperative education programmes and the employers who received them about the coop students. It was found that coop students' scores for written communication skills and problem-solving skills as learned skills during the coop experience was lower than other skills, which coincided with a low ratings of the students skills by coop employers. These findings are useful, so do the authors state, for improving the coop programme as well as informing the coop employers about the coop students thereby avoiding mismatches between the students and employers. It needs to be mentioned that the student data consisted of only those who experienced the programme, and thus it is not a comparison between those with and without the cooperative education programme. Consequently, it is more about how to evaluate the present programme rather than investigating the extra value the programme generates by its introduction.

Zegwaard and McCurdy (2008) asked 76 academic staff at science, engineering, computer, and mathematics facuilties at a New Zealand university a series of 19 questions about the effectiveness of work placement with a Likert data of five ranks from "strongly agree" (5 points) to "strongly disagree" (1 point). They found that the teachers felt with work placement, the students acquired hard and soft skills, but the effect on academic performance was not felt as much, and concluded that more extensive investigations and more involvement of the academic staff were indispensable. The analysis was based on creating a table of responses for the 19 questions and cross-examining the outcomes, and average points were directly compared to obtain the above conclusion.

Mendez (2008) looked at the relationship between industrial placements and final degree results of 80 engineering students at a British university in 2005 and 2007. He found the industrial placement has a positive effect on final degree. This study differs from Hartley and Smith (1999) and Zegwaard and McCurdy (2008) in that the data used are not a set of subjective response from the sampled academic staff, students, or employers but is a set of objective figures. Such investigation can offer more convincing opinion particularly when the validity of a project is in question. Mendez (2008) pointed out also that more extensive sampling and more rigorous statistical methodology may strengthen the argument for industrial placement.

These three studies all offer generally positive opinions about the effect of cooperative education. However, a more statistically rigorous investigation could have provided more convincing arguments. There are at least two issues to be worth considering. One is the sampling. All three studies are based on a sample rather than the entire body of students, or the population. Thus, one has to take into consideration some variations due to sampling condition – a sample does not always reflect the total population perfectly. Another issue is the standard by which investigators draw conclusion especially when one is dealing with numerical data – if, for example, two average final degree scores are compared, where should a dividing line be drawn between the real difference of the two groups and the sample variation?

These issues are somewhat solved in Heller and Heinemann (1987), Duignan (2003), and Van Gyn et al. (1996). Heller and Heinemann (1987) used a sample of 353 students from several colleges belonging to a university in United States to examine the effect of cooperative education on student's attitudes and values. Some of the findings include: those with work experience seem to be more dissatisfied with their jobs probably due to high expectation created by the experience, the coop students found their work experience to be satisfactory, and the coop students were more active about work preparation programmes at university. Although there is no explicit and systematic display of statistical testing, phrases such as "0.05 level of confidence" and "statistical significance" do suggest that the tests were used to verify if any clear difference exists between the coop student group and the non-coop student through questionnaires.

Duigan (2003) investigated the effects of placement on academic performance using data on over 150 student at a British university. Two types of work experience were subject of investigation. And he found that with a more extensive "learning environment model" students' academic performance significantly improved, while with a more basic "work environment model," the improvement was not observed. Furthermore, in both models, there was an evidence of "self-selection," that is, more academically competent students participated in the work placement. A series of t tests were used to see if there were significant differences in the academic performance between work placement group and non-work placement group.

Van Gyn et al. (1996) employed an analysis of variance or ANOVA on a sample of 999 engineering and art students from two Canadian universities to identify a gap in academic score between coop students and non-coop students. The ANOVA results showed that coop students perform better academically before and after participation in coop programme, implying that those who participate in coop programme are academically competent students in the first place. ANOVA is based on an F test and typically used in the present context to compare several averages, so that comparing two averages can be done with an F test. However, comparing of two averages can also be performed using a t test with an identical conclusion. Van Gyn et al. (1996) employed MANOVA, an analysis of variance on several traits. For example, a test score may be compared for coop students and non-coop students, male and female, faculties, and so on. In another words, MANOVA can trace identify several causes (independent variables) of the test score gap (dependent variable). In sum, ANOVA and MANOVA are much more powerful tools than a t test and a z test mentioned earlier. However, a simpler t test or a z test is sufficient to verify the difference between two values and a regression analysis would be more appropriate when these independent variables take continuous forms such as test scores and lengths of work experience rather than mere categories such as coop programme participation, gender, and faculty.

The rest of this section on existing studies with statistical analysis of cooperative education is spent on those based on a regression analysis. Gomez et al. (2004), Mendez and Rona (2011), and Foster et al. (2011) offer a standard linear regression analysis based on an ordinary least square method of estimation (OLS). They all use British data to verify the effect of work placement on final degree. Gomez et al. (2004) collected data from 164 bioscience students who graduated in 2001 or 2002. Average grade in the third and final year (L3 per cent) was regressed on gender (gender: 1 if male and 0 if female), pre-university academic score (HESAscore), average grade in the second year (L2 per cent), and work placement participation (mode: 1 if yes and 0 if no) to estimate a linear equation:

$$L3\% = a + b \, (\text{GENDER}) + c \, (\text{HESAscore}) + d \, (L2\%)$$
$$+ \, e \, (\text{mode}) + u \tag{5-1}$$

where u is an error term with OLS method. The result showed that all of these variables were positively significant in determining the third and final average grade (L3 per cent), as expected. Gomez et al. (2004) stressed the significance of work placement participation on academic performance.

Mendez and Rona (2010) ran a similar regression on a sample of 83 engineering students in a British university. Out of a similar set of independent variables as in Gomez et al. (2004), only the variables with statistically significance, namely the second year scores and industrial placement with both positive effect on final degree score, were kept – a procedure known as a *stepwise regression*. Having identified the quantitative relationship, Mendez and Rona (2010) stress a need for a qualitative investigation such as interviewing to clarify the mechanism of such causal relationship.

A word of caution may be required about a stepwise regression. It is a procedure to identify the most relevant independent variables among a set of potential independent variables. When a regression is ran, variables which show no significance, that is, low t-values or equivalently high P-values, are dropped at each step so that the final equation will have only those independent variables with significance. There is a mixed response to this procedure among statisticians and econometricians – while the former tend to approve (see, for example, Wonnacott and Wonnacott, 1990, or Ott and Longnecker, 2010), the latter tend to be skeptical about the procedure (see, for example, Wooldridge, 2009). Wooldridge (2009) argues that the selection of independent variables must be based on theoretical reasoning and not on what a particular set of data implies. And if an included independent variable shows no significance, it has to be shown in the estimated equation rather than leaving it out. This book shares this opinion about a stepwise regression.

Foster et al. (2011) estimated a linear causal relationship between degree performance and student's traits to find out about the effectiveness of work placement on final degree, with a sample of 530 business and economics students in a British university with work placement as an option between 2005 and 2011. The variables used were the same as those of Gomez et al. (2004). The estimation result was very similar except for the effect of pre-university academic scores, which did not show significance. The profound effect of work placement on academic performance made authors recommend its providers, that is, universities and employers, to make it easier for students to undertake work placement particularly in a tough economic climate.

Mandilaras (2004) analysed the effect of industrial placement on degree performance using data from 124 students of economics department at a British university. The analysis essentially followed the same procedure as that of Gomez et al. (2004) and Foster et al. (2011) apart from two distinct features. First, the set of independent variables included student's nationality – it is a dummy variable with 1 if the student is British and 0 otherwise. This was added because it was observed in the sample that British students slightly outperformed their non-British counterparts. Second, two types of dependent variable were used – average mark in the last 2 years, which is simply a positive value, and degree classification awarded upon graduation, which assigns 0 if uncompleted, 1 if a third class, 2 if a lower second class, up to a first class. The econometric model has to be different in the two cases. For the average marks, a linear equation was estimated with OLS, while a non-linear equation was estimated based on an ordered probit model – "probit" for qualitative response and "ordered" for the ranked response. The estimation results for both models show a similar tendency. In particular, placement experience, nationality, and a grade at earlier years were observed to have positive and significant effects on the later academic grade as well as on degree classification.

So far all the studies were concerned with the effectiveness of cooperative education, or equivalently, work experience, internship, or work placement on academic performance, while Gochenauer and Winter (2003) and McNabb et al. (2002) have slightly different foci but worth mentioning. Gochenauer and Winter (2003) investigated the effect of cooperative education not on academic performance but on employment outcomes after graduation. Their data consisted of 138 alumni of business studies at an American university, who graduated in 1998. A series of χ^2 tests and an OLS estimation were performed. The χ^2 tests showed that job satisfaction is not raised by internship experience, that internship experience shortened the time to obtain employment, and that the internship experience was considered to be worthwhile. An OLS estimation was performed with the salary for the first job as a dependent variable, being regressed on GPA, gender, subject major, and internship experience. Contrary to an expectation that these might show significant effect on salary, gender turned out to be the only significant factor – female respondents earned approximately $4000 less annually than the male counterparts, and neither GPA nor internship experience had any effect.

If the effects of education and cooperative education on economic life after graduation, one might have to wait a little while longer than just after graduation. It is so, because the realization of effect of education is not immediate but probably a lifelong process. However, the approach seems to have a right direction particularly with reference to human capital theory but perhaps requires a better data specification such as salary after 5 or 10 years rather than starting salary. It would be useful also to build the data consistently and consecutively.

McNabb et al. (2002) investigated whether educational attainment has gender difference. The data used were of the entire student population of 74,000 in United Kingdom, who left university in 1993. As in Mandilaras (2004), the educational attainment was expressed in terms of degree classification, and thus an ordered probit model was used for estimation. The main result reinforced a generally agreed fact that female students perform better academically on average, but the high achievers tended to be male. McNabb et al. (2002) explained that such result is caused by gender difference in attitude towards social success – male goes for the big success, while female weighs stability more. This study is added to the survey here for its rigorous treatment of data and clear presentation of estimation results. In particular, McNabb et al. (2002) has descriptive statistics to introduce a brief picture of variables used, explicit presentation of equations to be estimated, and the estimation result with all coefficients and corresponding t-values (or P values) irrespective of significant levels, and the sample size, some of which are sometimes missing in empirical works on cooperative education.

Table 5-1 summaries these 12 studies in terms of the main purpose, estimation method, sample characteristics, and result.

Table 5-1 The summary of the past studies of statistical analysis of the effectiveness of cooperative education (CE)

Author	Purpose	Method	Sample	Results
1 Hartley and Smith	2000 Effectiveness of CE	Direct comparisons	Students and employers asked about 57 coop students of management at a US university	Written communication skills and problem-solving skills needed to be reinforced. CE can be a catch for student recruitment. Informing coop employers about the students' characteristics. Inform academic admin the academic effect of CE.

2 Zegwaard and McCurdy	2008	Effect of CE on student performance	Direct comparisons	76 academic staff of science and engineering at a NZ university	Academics are not certain about the effectiveness. Need to inform them better.
3 Mendez	2008	Effect of CE on academic performance	Direct comparisons	80 engineering students at a British university in 2005 and 2007	Causal link to exist.
4 Heller and Heinemann	1987	Effect of CE on academic performances	Does not say, but probably t tests on difference in %	353 students from seven colleges of CUNY in 1984	The effect of CE is not clear.
5 Duignan	2003	Effect of CE on academic performance	t test and F test	100~200 students at a British university around 2000	Two types of placement: (1) Non-intensive pre-CE different but post-CE indifferent; (2) Intensive pre-CE different and post-CE different. And an evidence of self-selection, CE students do not improve from second to third year.
6 Van Gyn et al.	1996	Effect of CE and faculty on academic performance	ANOVA and MANOVA	999 engineering and art students at two Canadian universities	CE students are better academically before and after CE than others. Regression not possible as independent variables are categories and not values.
7 Gomez et al.	2004	Effect of CE on final degree	OLS	164 bioscience students at a British university	Final year grade influenced by gender, preU grade, second year grade, and CE.

(*Continued*)

Table 5-1 (Continued)

Author		Purpose	Method	Sample	Results
8 Mendez and Rona	2010	Effect of CE on final degree	Grade comparisons with t tests and stepwise regression	83 engineering students at a British university	CE as well as yr2 score have significant effects on final degree.
9 Foster et al.	2011	Effect of CE on final degree	OLS	530 business and economy students at a British university	Final degree influenced by second year grade, CE, gender but not PreU grades.
10 Mandrilaras	2004	Effect of CE on final degree	OLS for Grade and Ordered probit for Class	Economics students at a British university. Sample size unknown.	Final degree influenced by UK, A level Mathematics, CE, Grade in Yr2, no gender for economics students.
11 Gochnauer and Winter	2003	Effect of CE on employment outcomes	χ^2 test and OLS	138 alumni of business studies at a US university	CE useful for employment, but salary depends on gender and not on CE.
12 Nabb et al.	2002	Academic attainment and gender	Ordered probit	All students who left UK universities in 1993; 74,000	Females do better on average, but the high achievers tend to be males.

6   Hypothesis testing

t test, z test, χ^2 test, and ANOVA

This chapter introduces statistical tests to analyse the effectiveness of cooperative education. The hypothesis to test is whether there is a noticeable difference in certain outcomes between groups with and without cooperative education. Different tests are used for different types of data. Namely, a t test is used when a pair of numbers such as GPAs are compared, while z test or χ^2 test is used when a pair of proportions are compared. As briefly mentioned in the previous chapter, when comparing three or more means, analysis of variance (ANOVA) based on an F test needs to be used. But as the main focus of this book is the comparison of two types – coop and non-coop students – a simpler t test can be used, which gives the identical result to ANOVA.

(1)   Comparing means

Consider examining the effect of cooperative education on academic performance. Let GPA in the final year to represent the academic performance and pick up a given number of students at random, who may or may not have taken cooperative education programme. Then one can divide the students into those with and without cooperative education to compare the difference in GPA between the two groups. As GPA is likely to vary within each group, the comparison would be about the characteristics of the distributions of GPAs, with the most popular measure being the distribution's average. Consider a sample of 10 students with 4 coop students with GPAs 3.8, 3.5, 3.2, 2.4, and 6 non-coop students with GPAs 3.9, 3.5, 3.0, 2.9, 2.5, and 2.2 (see Table 6-1) – the example has a deliberately small size to show explicitly the calculation steps. This gives the average GPAs of 3.225 and 3.0. Is this difference large enough to conclude that cooperative education contributes to improve academic performance? There are two statistical issues to clarify before proceeding to the evaluation – namely, sampling and hypothesis testing.

The 10 GPA marks do not come from the whole group of students but a part of them or a "sample from the population." It follows then that it may not reflect the exact feature of the population depending of each pick. Consequently, the average or a "sample mean" out of the samples is not identical to the "population mean" of the entire students' body. Statistically, the sample

Table 6-1 The summary of the simple example with two groups

	With coop	Without coop	Total
	3.9	3.9	
	3.5	3.5	
	3.2	3.0	
	2.4	2.9	
		2.5	
		2.2	
Average GPA	$Xc = 3.225$	$Xnc = 3.0$	$X = 3.09$
Sample size	$Nc = 4$	$Nnc = 6$	$N = 10$

means have a distribution around the population mean with its own variance. This implies that when the difference of average GPA between coop and non-coop groups is compared by using the samples in the present example, the sample size needs to be taken into consideration, as this affects the reliability of the sampling and the type of distribution used for the test. The larger the sample is, the more information it conveys and thus the more reliable it will be. The distribution used for the test is called a t-distribution, but as the sample size increases, it approaches to a normal distribution. The rule of thumb is the sample size of 50 – use a t-distribution table for the size below 50 and a normal distribution table above 50.

The sample averages are compared to verify if there is no difference in the populations – or equivalently if they come from the same population. Formally, a null hypothesis that there is no difference in GPA between coop and non-coop groups is tested against an alternative hypothesis, which negates the former in one of the following ways: the averages differ, the average with coop is better, the average with coop is smaller. Some may think coop education raises the academic performance, while others may think it actually lowers it. A drawing line between accepting and rejecting the null hypothesis is expressed by a concept called a "significant level" or a "level of significance," which is generally set at 1 per cent, 5 per cent, or 10 per cent. This is the probability that the observed difference of sampling GPA averages is likely to accept the null hypothesis. So a significant level of, say, 5 per cent or less, means the probability of accepting the null hypothesis is lower than 5 per cent – that is, it is more likely to be non-zero or the GPAs for coop and non-coop groups are different. In the past, a statistical table of a standard normal distribution was used to compare the observed result with benchmark results corresponding to major significant levels such as 1 per cent, 5 per cent, and 10 per cent. But with an advancement in computer technology, one can easily calculate – for example with Excel, the exact significant level of the observation, and this is often denoted as a "P-value." Nowadays, statistical results are provided in either or both ways – with asterisks to indicate if the results exceed the significant levels at 1 per cent, 5 per cent, and 10 per cent, and/or with P-values. In this book, the former approach is adopted as in most of econometric works.

The statistical testing of the effect of coop education on academic performance of the above example would take the following steps.

(1) Set the null hypothesis (H0) and the alternative hypothesis (H1)

H0: GPAc = GPAnc, H1: GPAc ≠ GPAnc
where GPAc and GPAnc are the population averages for coop students and non-coop students respectively.

(2) Calculate the average of GPAs of the sampled coop students (Xc) and the average of GPAs of the sampled non-coop students (Xnc): Xc = 3.225, Xnc = 3.0

(3) Calculate the sum of squares of the differences between each GPA and the average for the two sets of samples: s^2c and s^2nc

where $s^2c = \sum(Xci - Xc)^2$
$= (3.8 - 3.225)^2 + (3.5 - 3.225)^2 + (3.2 - 3.225)^2 + (2.4 - 3.225)^2$
$= 1.0875$
and $s^2nc = \sum(Xnci - Xnc)^2$
$= (3.9 - 3.0)^2 + (3.5 - 3.0)^2 + (3.0 - 3.0)^2 + (2.9 - 3.0)^2 + (2.5 - 3.0)^2$
$+ (2.2 - 3.0)^2$
$= 1.960$

(4) Calculate the pooled variance of the two set of samples s^2:

where $s^2 = (s^2c + s^2nc)/(Nc + Nnc - 2) = (1.0875 + 1.96)/8 = 0.3809$

(5) Derive a value t (or t-statistic):

where $t = (Xc - Xnc)/s[\sqrt{(1/Nc + 1/Nnc)}]$
$= (3.225 - 3.0)/\sqrt{0.3809}\sqrt{[(1/4) + (1/6)]} = 0.5648$

(6) Use t to test H0 that the averages of GPAc and GPAnc are identical. The distribution to use for the test is a t-distribution with degree of freedom Nc + Nnc − 2 = 4 + 6 − 2 = 8. If t exceeds 1.86 (or 2.90), "the null hypothesis is rejected at a 5 per cent (1 per cent) significant level," that is, the coop students achieve a higher GPA than the non-coop students – or cooperative education raises the academic performance. (Note that more statistically rigorous phrase to express this result is "that cooperative education has no effect on academic performance is rejected.") Note that if t-value were negative, it would imply coop education has a negative effect on academic performance. As t is well below 1.86 (or 2.90), H0 is not rejected at 5 per cent (or 1 per cent) significant level, that is, the coop students do not achieve different GPAs from non-coop students.

The comparison of averages can also be performed by using ANOVA with the following steps:

(1) As for the t test
(2) As for the t test and also derive the average of all samples, X
(3) As for the t test
(4) As for the t test
(5) Calculate $Nc (Xc - X)^2 + Nnc (Xnc - X)^2 = 4x(3.225 - 3.09)^2 + 6x(3.0 - 3.09)^2$
    $= 0.1215$
(6) Derive a value F

> Where $F = Nc (Xc - X)^2 + Nnc (Xnc - X)^2 / s^2 = 0.1215/0.3809$
> $= 0.31898$

(7) Use F to test H0 that the averages of GPAc and GPAnc are identical. The distribution to use for the test is an F distribution with degrees of freedom 1 and $Nc + Nnc - 2 = 4 + 6 - 2 = 8$. If F exceeds 3.46 (or 8.41), "the null hypothesis is rejected at a 5 per cent (1 per cent) significant level," that is, the achieved GPAs by the coop and the non-coop students differ. Note that an F value is always positive, and on its own, it does not show which is greater – the inequality can be verified by comparing the average values themselves. As t is well below 3.46 (or 8.41), H0 is not rejected at 5 per cent (or 1 per cent) significant level, that is, the coop students do not achieve different GPAs from the non-coop students' GPA.

Note that this F value is equivalent to the t-value squared, that is, $F = 0.31898 = (0.5877)^2 = t^2$, where the t-distribution is with a degree of freedom 8 and ANOVA is equivalent to a two-tailed t test.

(2) Comparing proportions

The effect of cooperative education may also be measured by proportions as in the percentage of coop graduates in employment as opposed to being unemployed, in a full-time job as opposed to being in a part-time job, or in a listed company as opposed to being in a non-listed company. As in the previous example, the null hypothesis that cooperative education has no effect on these employment outcome would be tested against the alternative hypothesis that cooperative education improves the outcome. The testing procedure is almost identical to what has been discussed for two average values, except for the distribution and the variances. When a choice is binary, outcome follows a binomial distribution, and when the sample size is large enough, that is, a sample size n and proportion p satisfy $np > 5$ and $n(1 - p) > 5$, it becomes a normal distribution with a mean np and a variance $p(1 - p)$, where p is the probability of occurrence, following the central limit theory (Otto and Longnecker (2010)).

Table 6-2 Summary of a simple example with two groups

	Coop students	*Non-coop students*	*Total*
Full-time job	20	20	40
(Proportion)	Pc = 0.5	Pnc = 0.33	P = 0.4
Sample size	Nc = 40	Nnc = 60	N = 100

As a numerical example, let the sample of 100 graduates consist of 40 with coop experience and 60 without coop experience with both groups having 20 placed in full-time jobs. Let the sample size be N with Nc coop graduates and Nnc non-coop graduates, and the proportions of those graduates in the sample with full-time jobs for coop students and non-coop students be Pc and Pnc, while those in population be πc and πnc (see Table 6-2).

The statistical testing of the effect of coop education on a full-time job placement would take the following procedures. The steps are shown with the corresponding values for the above example.

(1) Set the null hypothesis (H0) and the alternative hypothesis (H1)

H0: $\pi c = \pi nc$, H1: $\pi c \neq \pi nc$

(2) Calculate the proportions of coop students and non-coop students at full-time jobs from the sample: Pc = 0.5 and Pnc = 0.33

(3) Calculate the total proportion of students at full-time jobs: P

where P = (PcNc + PncNnc)/(Nc + Nnc) = (0.5 × 40 + 0.33 × 60)/(40 + 60) = 0.4

(4) Derive a value z (or statistic):

where z = (Pc – Pnc)/$\sqrt{P(1 - P)(1/Nc + 1/Nnc)}$
= (0.5 – –0.33)/$\sqrt{0.4(1 - 0.4)(1/40 + 1/60)}$ = 1.67, given H0:
$\pi c = \pi nc$

(5) Use z to test H0 that $\pi c = \pi nc$. The distribution to use is a normal distribution. If z exceeds 1.64 (or 2.33), "the null hypothesis is rejected at a 5 per cent (1 per cent) significant level," that is, the coop students tend to be in full-time jobs more than the non-coop students. As z = 1.67 is greater than 1.64, implying H0 is rejected at a 10 per cent significance level, that is, the coop graduates have a higher chance of having full-time jobs than the non-coop graduates.

The comparison of proportions can also be tested using a χ^2 test, which is known as a *test of independence*. Let the observed numbers of coop graduates with full-time jobs and part-time jobs be a and b, while those of non-coop graduates be c and d. Table 6-3 is what is called a *contingency table* for the observed numbers.

Under the null hypothesis that there is no difference between the coop group and non-coop group – the outcome is "independent" of the group type. So if the "expected contingency table" under the null hypothesis has entries A, B, C, and D as in Table 6-4, then the following conditions has to be satisfied.

$$A = (a + b)(a + c)/(a + b + c + d) \tag{6-1}$$
$$B = (a + b)(b + d)/(a + b + c + d) \tag{6-2}$$
$$C = (a + c)(c + d)/(a + b + c + d) \tag{6-3}$$
$$D = (b + d)(c + d)/(a + b + c + d) \tag{6-4}$$

The test statistic χ^2 is defined as the sum of squared differences between the "observed values" and the "expected values under the null hypothesis" divided by the "observed figures." That is

$$\chi^2 = (a - A)^2/A + (b - B)^2/B + (c - C)^2/C + (d - D)^2/D \tag{6-5}$$

In the above example,

$$A = (a + b)(a + c)/(a + b + c + d) = (20 + 20)(20 + 20)/$$
$$(20 + 20 + 20 + 40) = 16 \tag{6-1'}$$
$$B = (a + b)(b + d)/(a + b + c + d) = (20 + 20)(20 + 40)/$$
$$(20 + 20 + 20 + 40) = 24 \tag{6-2'}$$

Table 6-3 Observed contingency table

	Full-time job	Part-time job	Total
Coop graduates	a	b	a + b
Non-coop graduates	c	d	c + d
Total	a + c	b + d	a + b + c + d

Table 6-4 Expected contingency table

	Full-time job	Part-time job
Coop graduates	A	B
Non-coop graduates	C	D

Table 6-5A Observed contingency table

Observed	Full-time job	Part-time job	Total
Coop graduates	20	20	40
Non-coop graduates	20	40	60
Total	40	60	100

Table 6-5B Expected contingency table

Expected	Full-time job	Part-time job	Total
Coop graduates	16	24	40
Non-coop graduates	24	36	60
Total	40	60	100

$$C = (a + c)(c + d)/(a + b + c + d) = (20 + 20)(20 + 40)/$$
$$(20 + 20 + 20 + 40) = 24 \qquad (6\text{-}3)'$$
$$D = (b + d)(c + d)/(a + b + c + d) = (20 + 40)(20 + 40)/$$
$$(20 + 20 + 20 + 40) = 36 \qquad (6\text{-}4)'$$

Therefor the observed and expected contingency tables for this example becomes as in Table 6-5 A and B.

Therefore,

$$\chi^2 = (20 - 16)^2/16 + (20 - 24)^2/24 + (20 - 24)^2/24 + (40 - 36)^2/36$$
$$= 25/9 = 2.78. \qquad (6\text{-}6)$$

The test for this type of contingency table with two rows and two columns is based on a χ^2 distribution with a degree of freedom 1, or $\chi^2_{(1)}$. The degree of freedom is 1, since fixing one of four entries in the contingency table, that is, A, B, C, and D, would determine all other entries given the observed numbers of coop graduates, non-coop graduates, those with full-time jobs, and those with part-time jobs. With a $\chi^2_{(1)}$ distribution table, 2.78 is greater than 2.71 for a 10 per cent significance level. Therefore, H0 is rejected at a 10 per cent significance level – in other words, cooperative education can be considered to influence the possibility of acquiring a full-time job.

Two tests can be used to verify the null hypothesis. In fact, the z test and the $\chi^2_{(1)}$ test are equivalent in the test for independence in a 2×2 contingency table, with $z^2 = \chi^2_{(1)}$. In the above example, $z^2 = 1.67^2 = 2.78 = \chi^2_{(1)}$. The difference is that when contingency table has more entries, z test cannot be used. Table 6-6 summarises the ways these tests can be used.

Table 6-6 When to use z test, t test, χ^2 test, and ANOVA

Quantity compared	Number of groups compared	Test and distribution used	Degree of freedom for 2 groups
Proportions	2	z test (Normal)	Not applicable
	2 or more	χ^2 test (χ^2)	1
Averages	2	t test (t)	n1 + n2 – 2
	2 or more	ANOVA (F)	1, n1 + n2 – 2

Note:
 (i) Degree of freedom only refer to cases when proportions or averages of two groups are compared – for ANOVA, n1 and n2 are sample sizes of the two groups.
 (ii) For comparing averages of two groups, a z test and a χ^2 test are equivalent.
 (iii) For comparing proportions of two groups, a t test and ANOVA are equivalent.

(3)   Testing the effect of cooperative education in Kyoto Sangyo University

Kyoto Sangyo University (KSU) has been gathering data on the subject registrations and marks of all students since early 2000s. The author of this book has been utilizing this data set to evaluate the effect of cooperative education in several occasions (See, for example, Tanaka, 2012; Tanaka and Carlson, 2012). The same data are used to illustrate the statistical testing methods of a z test, a t test, and a χ^2 test introduced earlier to compare the average GPAs and employment outcomes – whether the students find full-time or part-time jobs and whether the company is listed or unlisted, of those students with and without cooperative education. ANOVA is not used as it is not common as the other tests when two groups are compared.

This data set will be used throughout the rest of the book. Before that, a brief description is given on the Japanese university system and the development of cooperative education as well as on KSU and its student data set used.

The Japanese university system

The present Japanese educational system is based on the 6-3-3-4 system – 6 years of primary school, 3 years of junior high school, 3 years of senior high school, and 4 years of university, with the first 9 years, that is, primary and junior high school, being compulsory. The primary school starts at 6 years old and university completed at 22 years old, if continually attended throughout the education system. Kindergarten may be attended for 3 years previous to primary school. For higher education, there are also 2-year colleges (see Table 6-7). Academic year starts in April and ends in March of the following year for all schools and universities.

In 2009, when the data were collected, there were 773 universities, of which 178 were public and 595 were private, while there were 406 colleges, of which 28 were public and 378 were private, according to the School Basic Survey by the

Japanese Ministry of Education, Culture, Science and Technology (MEXT, 2009). In the same year, the student registration numbers were 2,845,908 for universities and 160,976 for colleges. The further breakdown of student number for universities and colleges into male and female and undergraduate and postgraduate shows that there are many more students at private than public universities, while for colleges, it is the opposite. There are more male university students, while there are more female college students, although the later has a much smaller size. Finally, there is a large body of undergraduate students, but only a small minority of undergraduate students proceed to postgraduate education – most undergraduate students seek for employment upon graduation (see Table 6-8).

Table 6-7 The main structure of the Japanese educational system

Age 3 4 5 6 7 8 9 10 11 12 13 14 15 16 17 18 19 20 21 22

x------------x-------------------------x----------------x--------------x------------------x

Kinder-	Primary school	Junior high	Senior high	University
garten		school	school	(College 2 yrs)
Pre-school	Primary education	Secondary education		Higher education

Note:
(i) Medicine and dentistry: 6 years
(ii) Postgraduate programmes: master's degree 2 years, doctoral degree (minimum of) 3 years
(iii) An academic year starts in April and ends in March of the following year.

Table 6-8 The number of schools and students in Japan (2009)

	University	*Colleges*
(Schools)		
Total	773	406
Public	178	28
Private	595	378
(Students)		
Total	2,845,908	160,976
Public	758,713	9,976
Private	2,087,195	151,000
Male	1,687,518	17,478
Female	1,158,390	143,498
Undergraduate	2,527,319	318,589
Postgraduate	160,976	0

Source: Basic School Survey (MEXT) (2009)

Table 6-9 The distribution of student number at university by subject in 2009

Humanities	Social Science	Science & Engineering	Medicine & Dentistry	Education	Others
15.4%	35.3%	24.3%	2.5%	6.3%	13.6%

Source: Basic School Survey (MEXT) (2009)

The same survey indicates that the distribution of undergraduate students by subject is rather unequal. More than half of them are in the non-science courses such as humanities, social science, and education as shown in Table 6-9.

The entry to university is not a privilege with an enrolment rate at 56.3 per cent with 57.3 per cent for male and 55.3 per cent for female, which shows a huge increase since the war even in the midst of the high economic growth of 1970s, the enrolment rate stood at 23.6 per cent with 29.2 per cent for male and 17.7 per cent for female. As for the exit from university, nowadays the students start job search while at university, and most of them have the job placement secured before graduation in March, so that they will start new jobs right after the graduation in the following April. This is one of the reasons why employment performance data can be gathered before graduation. This is, however, a "provisional" placement offer and could be cancelled under certain conditions including a case where the student fails to graduate. According to Japanese Ministry of Education, Culture, Science, Sports and Technology, this rate, a provisional job placement rate, among university graduates upon graduation has been above 90 per cent since 2000: 9 out of 10 university students graduate with a job in hand.

Development of cooperative education in Japan

Cooperative education is still a new concept in Japan. A similar concept of what is known as career education in Japan started drawing attention of educators and industrialists around the end of 1990s, particularly with the MEXT's introduction of the term in the "Report of Central Education Council" in 1999 (MEXT, 1999). A decade later in 2013, MEXT published a report on availability of internships, defined as programmes offering work experience, at universities as a part of career nurturing education programme (See Chapter 4). The report found that about 70 per cent of universities offer internships with academic credit attached and yet the actual percentage of students participating in any internship is as low as 2.2 per cent of the entire body of university students. It also points out that in 61.6 per cent of the cases, the duration of internship was less than mere 2 weeks. One hundred and sixty-one out of 526 universities, or about 31 per cent of them, reported that the internees were paid for their work, transport, or meals. It shows that the development of career-related (or henceforth cooperative) education in Japan is still far behind that of the advanced countries.

KSU and its cooperative education

KSU was founded in 1965 and is a medium sized private university in Japan with about 13,000 students in nine undergraduate faculties – Economics, Business Administration, Law, Foreign Languages, Cultural Studies, Science, Engineering, Computer Science and Engineering, and Life Science (at the time of the data collection in 2008 and 2009, there were seven faculties), and 200 students in eight graduate divisions – Economics, Economics Correspondence Education, Management, Law, Foreign Languages, Science, Engineering, and Frontier Informatics, and in Law School. At the time of the data collection, there were 20 cooperative education courses, of which 11 offered work-integrated learning programmes with direct contact with industry, while 9 offered induction programmes to introduce students to working life but without direct industrial contact.

The data set

The data has been collected from all 5,473 undergraduate students who graduated in 2008 and 2009 – 2,739 and 2,734 respectively. Of the total 5,473 students, 3,781 were male and 1,692 were female from seven faculties, that is, Economics, Business, Law, Foreign Languages, Culture, Science, and Engineering. From the original panel data of each student, the data on annual GPAs, whether he or she has taken cooperative education courses, and the employment outcome were used. Below is a brief description.

(i) The average annual GPAs for the first and third year of undergraduate courses, GPA1 and GPA3, are 1.90 and 1.90, respectively for total of 5,160 students out of 5,473, leaving out some with irregular registration patterns. GPA1 may be used to represent the student's academic ability before coming to university. This is because there is no standardized data on students' pre-university academic performance in Japan such as a national examination to cover every high school student and GPA1 is likely to depend on the pre-university achievement to great extent. GPA3 is used to identify the academic progress during the undergraduate years instead of the fourth year's GPA, due to a rather peculiar Japanese situation where many students manage to attain the necessary units to graduate by the end of third year to spend almost an entire fourth year for job search, so that their fourth year's GPA does not reflect their ability, as explained earlier.

(ii) Cooperative education: of 5,160 students considered in (i), 2,927 of them took at least one cooperative education course, while 2,233 took none. When the cooperative education courses are divided to work-integrated learning (WIL) courses and inductive courses, the former was taken by 692 students and the latter was taken by 2,235 students. Note that the percentage of students who took WIL is $692/5,160 = 13.4$ per cent, which is much higher than the national average of 2.2 per cent.

(iii) Employment outcome: This was measured form two angles. First, the students were asked whether they have obtained "provisional placement offers" of full-time employment, part-time employment, or none. Out of 5,160 students, 4,195 obtained full-time employment offers, while 421 obtained part-time employment offers. Second, 3,965 offers students received were from private companies with 1,354 listed companies and 2,611 unlisted companies. It needs to be mentioned that considering the history and nature of KSU, it is probably a typical Japanese private university. Thus, the statistical analysis of KSU may well be consistent with what other university would find if a similar analysis is made.

Testing the effect of cooperative education at KSU

Given the above information, the following section illustrates how to test the effectiveness of cooperative education at KSU. The statistical testing will be performed on the three definitions of cooperative education: cooperative education, WIL, and induction courses. The students will be divided into those with and without cooperative education and the academic and employment outcomes of the two groups are compared.

(i)   Effect of cooperative education on GPA1 and GPA3

There were 5,160 students divided into two groups in the following three ways: those with and without cooperative education, those with and without WIL, and those with and without induction courses. The average GPAs were found as in Table 6-10.

With the procedure illustrated earlier in this chapter, the existence of a significant difference in an academic performance level between students groups with and without cooperative education is tested using a t test (not ANOVA since they give equivalent result as verified earlier), and the following results are found (although the full steps are not given here, in

Table 6-10 Average GPAs by group

	Student number	Average GPA1	Average GPA3
With cooperative education	2,927	1.96	1.95
Without cooperative education	2,233	1.81	1.83
With WIL	692	2.17	2.2
Without WIL	4,468	1.85	1.85
With induction courses	2,235	1.9	1.87
Without induction courses	2,925	1.89	1.91

order to show the calculation process the actual values used to derive t-value are provided in the note):

(a) Question: Are average GPA1s of groups with and without cooperative education, 1.96 and 1.81, significantly different?

Answer: t = 7.85, which means they are significantly different at 1 per cent. (P-value = 0)
   Note: t = $(1.96 - 1.81)/s[\sqrt{(1/2927 + 1/2233)}]$
   where s^2 = $(1288.37 + 1096.91)/(2927 + 2233 - 2) = 0.462$

(b) Question: Are average GPA3s of groups with and without cooperative education, 1.95 and 1.83, significantly different?

Answer: t = 6.22, which means they are significantly different at 1 per cent. (P-value = 0)
   Note: t = $(1.95 - 1.83)/s[\sqrt{(1/2927 + 1/2233)}]$
   where s^2 = $(1346.36 + 1083.17)/(2927 + 2233 - 2) = 0.471$

(c) Question: Are average GPA1s of groups with and without WIL, 2.17 and 1.85, significantly different?

Answer: t = 11.59, which means they are significantly different at 1 per cent. (P-value = 0)
   Note: t = $(2.17 - 1.85)/s[\sqrt{(1/692 + 1/4468)}]$
   where s^2 = $(274.52 + 2081.53)/(692 + 4468 - 2) = 0.457$

(d) Question: Are average GPA3s of groups with and without WIL, 2.2 and 1.85, significantly different?

Answer: t = 12.62, which means they are significantly different at 1 per cent. (P-value = 0)
   Note: t = $(2.2 - 1.85)/s[\sqrt{(1/692 + 1/4468)}]$
   where s^2 = $(339.4 + 2037.38)/(692 + 4468 - 2) = 0.461$

(e) Question: Are average GPA1s of groups with and without induction courses, 1.9 and 1.89, significantly different?

Answer: t = 0.52, which means they are not significantly different. (P-value = 0.603)
   Note: t = $(1.9 - 1.89)/s[\sqrt{(1/2235 + 1/2925)}]$
   where s^2 = $(975.25 + 1440.62)/(2235 + 2925 - 2) = 0.468$

(f) Question: Are average GPA3s of groups with and without induction courses, 1.87 and 1.91, significantly different?

Answer: t = –2.07, which means they are significantly different at 5 per cent. (P-value = 0.039)
   Note: t = $(1.96 - 1.81)/s[\sqrt{(1/2927 + 1/2233)}]$
   where s^2 = $(1288.37 + 1096.91)/(2927 + 2233 - 2) = 0.474$

These test results seem to suggest that, when cooperative education as a whole or WIL is used to test the difference in students' academic quality, it attracts better students, that is students with higher GPA1s and also it makes them perform better academically at university, that is students with higher GPA3. However, when students are grouped by whether participating induction courses, there seems to be no academic difference between the groups at pre-university level, that is, the GPA1 difference is not significant. As for GPA3, those with induction courses seem to perform "not better but worse," and the result is significant. One possible explanation is the induction courses are rather basic courses, and more academically advanced students may not take them.

(ii)   Effect of cooperative education on obtaining a full-time/part-time job

There were 4,616 students divided into two groups in the following three ways: those with and without cooperative education, those with and without WIL, and those with and without induction courses. The number of students in each category is shown in Table 6-11.

With the procedure illustrated earlier in this chapter, the existence of a significant difference in a job status between students groups with and without cooperative education is tested using a z test and a $\chi^2_{(1)}$ test – as pointed earlier in this chapter, they give the identical test result, and the following results are found (the results are shown with corresponding calculation process and the contingency tables for observed and expected values).

(a) Question: Does cooperative education improve the chance of getting a full-time job?

Answer 1: z test

z = 6.46, which means cooperative education significantly improves a chance of getting a full-time job.

Table 6-11 Job placement status by group

	Full-time	Part-time	Full-time (%)
Total	4,195	421	90.9%
With cooperative education	2,516	184	93.2%
Without cooperative education	1,679	237	87.6%
With WIL	621	20	96.9%
Without WIL	3,574	401	89.9%
With induction courses	1,895	164	92.0%
Without induction courses	2,300	257	89.9%

Note: $z = (0.932 - 0.876)/\sqrt{[0.909 (1 - 0.909)(1/2700 + 1/1916)]} = 6.46$

Answer 2: χ^2 with one degree of freedom

Contingency tables for observed values and expected vales are

	Observed Full-time/Part-time		Expected Full-time/Part-time	
With cooperative education	2,516	184	2,454	246
Without cooperative education	1,679	237	1,741	175

Thus $\chi^2 = (2516 - 2454)^2/2454 + (184 - 246)^2/246 + (1679 - 1741)^2/ 1741 + (237 - 175)^2/175 = 41.72 = 6.46^2 = z^2$

In both cases, the effect is significant at 1 per cent. (P-value $= 0$)

(b) Question: Does WIL improve the chance of getting a full-time job?

Answer 1: z test

$z = 5.67$, which means cooperative education significantly improves a chance of getting a full-time job.

Note: $z = (0.969 - 0.899)/\sqrt{[0.909 (1 - 0.909)(1/641 + 1/3975)]} = 5.67$

Answer 2: χ^2 with one degree of freedom

Contingency tables for observed values and expected vales are

	Observed Full-time/Part-time		Expected Full-time/Part-time	
With WIL	621	20	583	58
Without WIL	3,574	401	3,612	363

Thus $\chi^2 = (621 - 583)^2/583 + (20 - 58)^2/58 + (3574 - 3612)^2/3612 + (401 - 363)^2/363 = 32.33 = 5.67^2 = z^2$

In both cases, the effect is significant at 1 per cent. (P-value $= 0$)

(c) Question: Do induction courses improve the chance of getting a full-time job?

Answer 1: z test

$z = 2.45$, which means cooperative education significantly improves a chance of getting a full-time job.

Note: $z = (0.920 - 0.899)/\sqrt{[0.909 (1 - 0.909)(1/2557 + 1/2059)]} = 2.45)$

Answer 2: χ^2 with one degree of freedom

Contingency tables for observed values and expected vales are

	Observed Full-time/Part-time		Expected Full-time/Part-time	
With induction courses	1,895	164	1,871	188
Without induction courses	2,300	257	2,324	233

Thus $\chi^2 = (1895 - 1871)^2/1871 + (164 - 188)^2/188 + (2300 - 2324)^2/$
$\qquad 2324 + (257 - 233)^2/233 = 5.99 = 2.45^2 = z^2$

In both cases, the effect is significant at 1 per cent. (P-value = 0.0142)

(iii)   Effect of cooperative education on obtaining a job at a listed/unlisted company

There were 3,965 students divided into two groups in the following three ways: those with and without cooperative education, those with and without WIL, and those with and without induction courses. The number of students in each category is shown in Table 6-12.

(a) Question: Does cooperative education improve the chance of getting a job at a listed company?

Answer 1: z test
z = 1.60, which means cooperative education may not significantly improve a chance of getting a full-time job.
Note: $z = (0.351 - 0.326)/\sqrt{[0.341 (1 - 0.341)(1/2412 + 1/1553)]} = 1.60$
Answer 2: χ^2 with one degree of freedom
Contingency tables for observed values and expected vales are

	Observed Listed/Unlisted		Expected Listed/Unlisted	
With cooperative education	847	1,565	824	1,588
Without cooperative education	507	1,046	530	1,023

Thus $\chi^2 = (847 - 824)^2/824 + (1565 - 1588)^2/1588 + (507 - 530)^2/$
$\qquad 530 + (1046 - 1023)^2/1023 = 2.56 = 1.60^2 = z^2$

In both cases, the effect is not significant. (P-value = 0.11)

Table 6-12 Company status by group

	Listed	Unlisted	Listed (%)
Total	1,354	2,611	34.1%
With cooperative education	847	1,565	35.1%
Without cooperative education	507	1,046	32.6%
With WIL	221	372	37.3%
Without WIL	1,133	2,239	33.6%
With induction courses	626	1,193	34.4%
Without induction courses	728	1,418	33.9%

(b) Question: Does WIL improve the chance of getting a job at a listed company?

Answer 1: z test

z = 1.74, which means cooperative education significantly improves a chance of getting a full-time job.

Note: $z = (0.372 - 0.336)/\sqrt{[0.341 (1 - 0.341)(1/593 + 1/3372)]} = 1.74$

Answer 2: χ^2 with one degree of freedom

Contingency tables for observed values and expected vales are

	Observed Listed/Unlisted		Expected Listed/Unlisted	
With cooperative education	221	372	203	390
Without cooperative education	1,133	2,239	1,151	2,221

Thus $\chi^2 = (221 - 203)^2/203 + (372 - 390)^2/390 + (1133 - 1151)^2/1151 + (2239 - 2221)^2/2221 = 3.02 = 1.74^2 = z^2$

In both cases, the effect is significant at 10 per cent. (P-value = 0.08)

(c) Question: Do induction courses improve the chance of getting a job at a listed company?

Answer 1: z test

z = 0.32, which means cooperative education does not significantly improves a chance of getting a full-time job.

Note: $z = (0.344 - 0.339)/\sqrt{[0.341 (1 - 0.341)(1/1819 + 1/2146)]} = 0.32$

Answer 2: χ^2 with one degree of freedom

Contingency tables for observed values and expected vales are

	Observed Listed/Unlisted		Expected Listed/Unlisted	
With cooperative education	626	1,193	621	1,198
Without cooperative education	728	1,418	733	1,413

Thus $\chi^2 = (626 - 621)^2/621 + (1193 - 1198)^2/1198 + (728 - 733)^2/733 + (1418 - 1413)^2/1413 = 0.106 = 0.32^2 = z^2$

In both cases, the effect is not significant. (P-value = 0.745)

In sum, the following conclusion can be drawn:

(1) When students are grouped into those with and without cooperative education, as well as with and without WIL, the averages of first year and third year GPA are both significantly higher for the former group.
(2) When students are grouped into those with and without induction courses, the averages of first year GPA of the two groups show no significant

difference, while the average of third year GPA for the former group shows significantly lower result.

(3) When students are grouped into those with and without cooperative education, with and without induction courses and with and without WIL, the percentage of getting a full-time job is always significantly higher for the former group.

(4) The effects of cooperative education is not significantly felt for obtaining a job at a listed company except for WIL.

(5) One may conclude that generally cooperative education has a positive effect on academic performance and employment outcome. However, it does suggest also that students who take cooperative education and WIL in particular have high per-university academic performance. If it is true, then value of cooperative education is overestimated. The next chapter deals with this issue of singling out the effect of cooperative education, by using regression analysis

7 Constructing a framework for regression analysis

The interactive mechanism of attributes of a student, who receives cooperative education and then finds employment upon graduation, was described by the path diagram in Figure 5-1 of Chapter 5. It was also pointed out in the chapter that a theoretical framework known as path analysis can be built, by which the causal links among the attributes are statistically tested. This chapter introduces a set of hypotheses based on the causal relationships in the path diagram and the econometric framework to test these hypotheses.

(1) Path analysis and six hypotheses

The causal relationships in Figure 5-1 can be expressed as

PreU → CE	(7-1)
PreU & CE → Acad	(7-2)
PreU, CE, & Acad → Emp	(7-3)

where "→" indicates the causal relationship.

  PreU is *pre-university background:* an academic performance before coming to university.
  CE is *reinforcement I:* whether or not cooperative education is taken or quantity of cooperative education taken.
  Acad is *reinforcement II:* an academic performance at university.
  Emp is *economic outcome:* an employment outcome such as employment status or company status.

Verifying each of these causal relationships becomes crucial for evaluating university education system in various ways (see Figure 7-1, which is reproduced from Figure 5-1 with the new terms). Those engaged in cooperative education programme would like to know how effective it is to improve academic performance and employment outcomes (i.e. V and IV). For those in academic programme, it is important to know how effective it is (i.e. IV). No strong causal tie between pre-university and

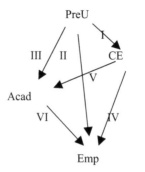

Figure 7-1 Path diagram from higher school to job through higher education

university academic performances may imply that the university provides every student equal opportunity to develop academically, irrespective of academic background (i.e. III). As for those who seek social recognition of university such administrative members, how academic performance affects employment outcome (i.e. VI) and how pre-university academic performance affects employment outcome (i.e. II) may matter the most. For the former, a strong causal relationship could be implied to prove their academic programme is answering to society's employment needs, while for the latter, a weak causal relationship could imply a university providing equal opportunity to study and develop to earn employment opportunity. For cooperative education, a strong causal relationship from pre-university academic performance to cooperative education participation (i.e. I) could discount its effectiveness, since this could mean cooperative education programme "simply attracted" high-academic achievers.

In the following three chapters, empirical work is conducted using student data from Kyoto Sangyo University and Hong Kong Polytechnic University to verify six hypotheses, each corresponding to the arrows in Figure 7-1.

> Hypothesis I: Pre-university academic performance affects cooperative education participation (i.e. PreU → CE).
> Hypothesis II: Pre-university academic performance affects employment outcome (i.e. PreU → Emp).
> Hypothesis III: Pre-university academic performance affects academic performance at university (i.e. PreU → Acad).
> Hypothesis IV: Cooperative education affects employment outcome (i.e. CE → Emp).
> Hypothesis V: Cooperative education affects academic performance at university (i.e. CE → Acad).
> Hypothesis VI: Academic performance at university affects employment outcome (i.e. Acad → Emp).

These hypotheses and the causal relationships may be expressed in linear equations for estimation as below (see (2) below if the dependent variable takes 1 or 0 value) with an added error term uncorrelated to each other:

Equation I: CE = a1 + b1 PreU + u1 (Hypothesis I) (7-1)'
Equation II: Acad = a2 + b2 PreU + c2 CE + u2
(Hypotheses III and V) (7-2)'
Equation III: Emp = a3 + b3 PreU + c3 CE + d3 Acad + u3
(Hypotheses II, IV, and VI) (7-3)'

When variables appear in more than one equation in the set of equations, the framework is referred to as a *structural equation model* or a *simultaneous equation model,* as briefly explained in Chapter 5. In particular, when the set of equation forms a hierarchical or a triangular structure as (7-1) to (7-3), it is called a *fully recursive model,* and an ordinary least square (OLS) method may be used to estimate coefficients of each equation, that is, a's, b's, and c's, separately; the OLS estimator is said to be a "consistent" estimator, that is, unbiased for a large sample size (see, for example Brooks, 2008; Greene, 2008; Wooldridge, 2009 and 2010). The data specification and estimation procedures for the three equations are described below in turn.

(2) Background of cooperative education students

Equation I: CE = a1 + b1 PreU + u1 (Hypothesis I) (7-1)'

This equation estimates the effect of pre-university academic performance on the decision to take cooperative education. As pointed earlier, it is possible that those students who are interested in cooperative education were already academically motivated before stating university career. Higher school grades can be used to represent pre-university academic performance if any national data are available. If, however, no such exam exists or cannot be traced to cover all the students concerned, the best proxy would be their grades, for example GPA, in the first term or first year at university, since this result is more likely to be a reflection of pre-university achievement rather than what is achieved at university. CE could be a variable that is 1 if cooperative education course is taken and 0 otherwise. But this can be a problem if the data are collected from a particular university where cooperative education is mandatory. In such a case, a quantitative measure such as a total length of work experience, a number of coop companies the student had work experience with, or a number of cooperative education related courses taken can be used. The decision to follow cooperative education programme may also depend on student's other personal attributes such as gender or faculty that he or she belongs. Thus, the equation to estimate may be rewritten as

CE = a1 + b1 PreU + m1 Faculty + n1 Gender + u1 (7-1)"

where, the dependent variable, CE takes a positive value and the independent variables, PreU may be grades, and Faculty and Gender are dummies.

A straightforward OLS estimation may be applied, when CE is a quantitative variable such as a length of work experience or a number of cooperative education-related courses taken. However, if CE is a one/zero variable, such a model is called *a binary response model.* This belongs to a family of *limited dependent variable models,* in which the range of values of dependent variable is substantially limited. In some cases, an assumption of a linear equation or a straightforward use of an OLS method may not be appropriate.

For binary response models, the causal relationship in (7-1) is expressed as

$$\text{Prob}(\text{CE} = 1) = F(a1 + b1 \text{ PreU}) \qquad\qquad (7\text{-}1)'''$$

where Prob(CE = 1) is the probability of a student with a given PreU taking cooperative eudcation or CE = 1, and F is its functional form with a linear probablity, a logit model, or a probit model as the most common. For estimation, it becomes

$$\text{CE} = F(a1 + b1 \text{ PreU}) + u1 \qquad\qquad (7\text{-}1)''''$$

since what is observed is CE = 1 or 0 and not the probability, which is called a latent variable (The discussion to follow can be found in most of standard textbooks of econometrics – for example, see Wooldridge, 2009).

The linear probability model expresses the probability of response as a linear function of independent variables as in (7-1)'. However, it has a theoretical flaw that the predicted values of dependent variable may lie outside of the 0–1 range for extreme values of independent variables (see Figure 7-2). The binary nature of dependent variable also implies non-uniform or heteroskedastic errors. In this case, OLS estimators are not biased but for t and F statistics, the usual standard errors

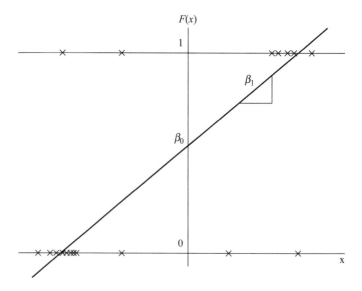

Figure 7-2 A graph of a linear probability model with a single independent variable

need to be replaced by *heteroskedasticity-robust standard errors,* since the error terms are not normally distributed. In practice, however, these error values are not far from each other. Besides, the estimation procedure for this model is simple as OLS is used for the linear equation directly and the interpretation of the coefficients is intuitive – an increase in a unit values of a variable would raise the probability of taking CE by the estimated coefficient. If it is a dummy variable, its coefficient tells the gap in probability between the variable and the reference category (or the base group) – for example, if 1 for male and 0 for female, then female is the reference category (see more extended explanation in the next section on Equation II).

Unlike a linear probability model, a logit model keeps the dependent variable between 0 and 1. The term *logit* comes from *a logistic curve* (see Figure 7-3). If the probability of response p = Prob (CE =1) depends on x linearly, that is, ax + b, then a logistic curve is expressed by

$$p = \exp(ax + b)/[1 + \exp(ax + b)] \tag{7-4}$$

It can be easily verified that if ax + b approaches ∞ (or – ∞), p approaches 1 (or 0).

The equation can be rearranged in a linear form by a logit transformation as

$$\ln p/(1 - p) = ax + b \tag{7-5}$$

This could be estimated by a least square method if p takes values other than 1 or 0. In the present case, where the dependent variable takes 1 or 0, it is not feasible, but when the probability is replaced by an observed percentage such as the average percentage of those who have taken the choice for each group, the least square method can be used, and it is known as a *minimum χ² method.*

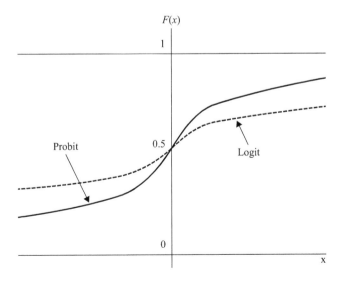

Figure 7-3 Graphs of a logit model and a probit model with a single independent variable

A probit model is based on the standard normal cumulative distribution and can be expressed as

$$p = (2\pi)^{-1/2} \int_{-\infty}^{ax+b} \exp(-z^2/2) \, dz \qquad (7\text{-}6)$$

It can be verified that, as in the logit model above, if $ax + b$ approaches ∞ (or $-\infty$), $p = \text{Prob}(CE = 1)$ approaches 1 (or 0).

As both logit and probit are non-linear in $ax + b$ unlike the linear probability model, so (7-1) cannot be used as an estimated equation and some cautions are needed for the estimation process. First, a straightforward least square method would not work because of the non-linearity. For the non-linear estimation, most commonly used method today is the *maximum likelihood estimation*. Second, the estimated coefficients do not give a straightforward interpretation of the least square estimation, since a unit increase of an independent variable will cause a marginal change in the dependent variable through the non-linear forms of the logit and probit equations. This means that the estimated coefficients of the linear probability, logit, and probit models cannot be directly compared. There is a further complication that for the logit and probit models, these values depend on the values of independent variables – note that for the linear probability model, the marginal effect is constant over the values of independent variables. In order to make the estimated coefficients of the three models comparable, they may be multiplied by a *scale factor* defined either as the average partial effect (APE) or the partial effect at average (PEA), which are calculated using average values over the observed independent variables. Alternatively, as a rule of thumb, Wooldridge (2009) suggests using scale factors to multiply the coefficients for the logit and probit models of 0.4 and 0.25 respectively, to compare directly the coefficients among the three models. Also, as a statistic for goodness-of-fit or adjusted R^2 in the least square method, McFadden (1974) suggested a statistic known as "Pseudo R^2" for the maximum likelihood method, which is often found in statistical packages. Table 7-1 below summarizes the estimation characteristics of the three models described above.

Table 7-1 The comparison of the three binary response models: Linear Probability, Logit, and Probit

a. Estimated model	Linear Probability	Logit	Probit
b. Estimated equation	Linear	Non-linear	Non-linear
c. Estimation method	OLS	MLE	MLE
d. t-value	Hetreoskedastisity –robust t	t	t
e. R^2	Adjusted R^2	Pseudo R^2	Pseudo R^2
f. Effect on CE	Coefficient	Marginal effect	Marginal effect
g. Advantage	Simplicity and intuitiveness	Theoretical rigour	Theoretical rigour
h. Disadvantage	Theoretical inconsistency	Theoretical complexity	Theoretical complexity

Note: Ordinary least square (OLS); Maximum likelihood (MLE)

(3)   Causes of good academic performance

Equation II: Acad = a2 + b2 PreU + c2 CE + u2   (7-2)'

The dependent variable Acad, is academic performance at university. As CE is assumed to depend on CE, and CE is often taken in the middle years of undergraduate programme, GPA in the final year or final term would be an appropriate variable. The equation can take a linear form, as it is a quantitative variable. The independent or marginal effects of PreU and CE on Acad are estimated. Again CE can take different forms and several equations with different definitions of CE may be estimated. And individual attributes of a student such as faculty and gender may be added to redefine Equation II as

Equation II: Acad = a2 + b2 PreU + c2 CE + m2 Faculty + n2
Gender + u2   (7-2)"

A usual least square method works in this case due to the quantitative nature of Acad and the linearity of the equation. Suppose PreU is given by high school grade and Acad by the final year GPA. A coefficient on PreU, b2, would show how much increase in the final year's GPA is brought about by an increase in a unit of the high school grade if other variables remain unchanged. Other variables in Equation II, that is, CE, Faculty, and Gender, are dummy variables, and their estimated coefficients tell how much that particular trait influences the dependent variable. Thus, if the gender variable is defined with 1 if male and 0 if female, then the estimated coefficient tells how much difference in the final year GPA exists between male and female students with other attributes being identical. If there are more than two categories as in Faculty, the number of dummy variables will be one less than the number of categories. The variable that does not appear in the equation is called a *reference category* or a *base group,* and the estimated coefficient on each of the dummy variables tells the difference in how the variable influences the dependent variable relative to the base group.

To illustrate how to interpret an estimation result of an OLS on a linear equation, consider a following equation,

GPAfinal = a2 + b2 HSgr c2 CE + m11 FacultyE + m12
FacultyB + n1Gender + u1   (7-7)

where GPAfinal is the GPA in the final year at university, HSgr is the high
   school grade before entering university, and CE is a dummy variable with 1
   if cooperative education course is taken and 0 otherwise.
Faculty is a faculty dummy for three faculties – Economics, Business, and
   Law,
   and if a student is from Economics, then FacultyE =1, and FacultyB = 0;
   if a student is from Business, then FacultyE = 0, and FacultyB = 1; and
   if a student is from Law, then FacultyE = 0, and FacultyB = 0.
Gender is a dummy variable with 1 if male and 0 if female.

Now suppose running an ordinary least square estimation on this equation gives the following result:

$$\text{GPAfinal} = 3.4 + 0.59 \text{ HSgr} + 0.12 \text{ CE} + 0.21 \text{ FacultyE} -$$
$$(3.5) \quad (4.1) \qquad (1.2) \qquad (2.1)$$
$$-0.32 \text{ FacultyB} - 0.11 \text{ Gender} \quad \text{(t-values in parenthesis)}$$
$$(-0.2) \qquad\qquad\qquad (-2.5) \qquad \text{Adjusted } R^2 = 0.62 \qquad (7\text{-}8)$$

Each coefficients explains the effect of corresponding variable on the dependent variable if all other variables remain unchanged. Thus, the coefficient of 0.59 on HSgr means GPAfinal is higher by 0.59 for a student with one unit higher HSgr, with the same CE, Faculty, and Gender. The coefficient of 0.12 on CE means those with cooperative education on average attain 0.12 higher GPAfinal than the non-cooperative education counterpart given that all other variables are identical. The coefficient of –0.11 on Gender means a male student with the same HSgr, CE, and faculty has 0.11 lower GPAfinal than the female counterpart. The first faculty coefficient of 0.21 implies that a student with given HSgr, CE, and Gender in the faculty of economics has 0.21 higher GPAfinal than a student in the law faculty, which is the base group. Similarly, the second faculty coefficient of –0.32 implies that a student with given HSgr, CE, and gender in the faculty of business has 0.32 lower GPAfinal than the law faculty counterpart. The t-values (or t-statistics) with parentheses below the coefficients tell how many standard deviations away the estimated values from 0, that is the null hypothesis, in the standard normal distribution, as in the comparison of averages and proportions in the earlier chapter. Thus the larger t-value is, the more likely it is that the estimated coefficients are meaningful. The corresponding P-values can be calculated but they also depend on the sample size. However, as a rule of thumb t-value of more than 2 or less than –2 implies that the estimated coefficient is a reliable value. For the above example, the estimated coefficients for CE and FacultyB are not reliable, that is, more likely to be zero. Adjusted R^2 examines the power of the equation to explain the causal relationship. In the above case, this linear equation with given independent variables can explain 62 per cent of the causal relationship. The remaining unexplained 38 per cent may be due to excluding appropriate variables or to a wrong functional form – for example, it may not be linear. Another common statistic, although not displayed here, is F-value (or F-statistic), which is used to test if the all coefficients are 0, that is there is no causal relationship, and the bigger value would mean, as in the case of t-value, to negate the null hypothesis.

(4)   Causes of successful employment outcome

Equation III: $\text{Emp} = a3 + b3 \text{ PreU} + c3 \text{ CE} + d3 \text{ Acad} + u3$ $\qquad (7\text{-}3)'$

The dependent variable Emp is the quality of job placement or self-evaluation of job performance. The quality of job placement may be defined either by the job status, that is, full-time or part-time, or by the company status, that is, listed or unlisted, of one's first job. Or the self-evaluation data could be collected by sending out questionnaires to alumni after several years of employment. However, Emp is a discrete variable as CE in Equation I and thus the same response model approach needs to be taken with a linear probability, a logit, and a probit models to be estimated by the OLS method for the first and the maximum likelihood estimation method for the other two. Here, also a set of individual attributes may be added and Equation III will become

Equation III: Emp = F (a3 + b3 PreU + c3 CE + d3 Acad
+ m3 Faculty + n3 Gender) + u3   (7-3)"

The difficulty here is that the employment variables are not obtainable while the students are at university, and one may find it difficulty or costly to collect such data.

The following three chapters test the Hypotheses I to VI by using these estimation methods on student and alumni data from Kyoto Sangyo University and Hong Kong Polytechnic University.

8 Who takes cooperative education programme?

As it has been noted earlier, students may not decide to take cooperative education programme at random, but there may be a tendency among certain group of students to do so. In the previous chapter, Equation I of the path analysis illustrated such a tendency with

$$CE = a1 + b1 \text{ PreU} + m1 \text{ Faculty} + n1 \text{ Gender} + u1 \qquad (7\text{-}1)"$$

which says that whether a student takes cooperative education programme depends on the student's attributes such as pre-university academic performance, gender, and faculty. In another words, an academically motivated high school leaver might be more interested in cooperative education programme, it might have a gender difference, and it might be the faculty which encourages or discourages the programme due to its curriculum policy. This chapter shows how one can proceed to verify such statements with a particular interest in the first of the three statements or:

> Hypothesis I: Pre-university academic performance affects cooperative education participation

The Kyoto Sangyo University (KSU) student data are used with the econometric methodology discussed in Chapter 7. The analysis of Chapter 8 is based on and extended from Tanaka (2012).

(1) KSU data and development of cooperative education in Japan

This come from the same data source used in Chapter 6, and a brief and selected summary of the data relevant to this chapter is given below.

KSU was founded in 1965 and is a medium-sized private university in Japan with about 13,000 students in nine undergraduate faculties – Economics, Business Administration, Law, Foreign Languages, Cultural Studies, Science, Engineering, Computer Science and Engineering, and Life Science (at the time of the data collection in 2008 and 2009, there were seven faculties), and 200 students in eight graduate divisions. At the time of the data collection, there were 20 cooperative education courses, of which 11 offered work-integrated learning programmes with direct contact with industry, while 9 offered induction programmes to introduce students to working life but without direct industrial contact.

The data have been collected from all 5,473 undergraduate students who graduated in March of 2008 and 2009 – 2,739 and 2,734 respectively. Of the total 5,473 students, 3,781 were male and 1,692 were female from seven faculties – Economics with 1,265 students, Business with 1,291, Law with 1,173, Foreign Languages with 802, Cultural studies with 446, Science with 282, and Engineering with 214. From the original panel data of each student, the data used for the econometric analysis include annual GPAs, whether and how many cooperative education courses have been taken, and the employment outcome, as well as the student's gender and faculty, as explained below.

(i) Annual GPAs over 4 years: the average annual GPAs for the 4 years of undergraduate courses are 1.90, 1.74, 1.90, and 1.53. The first year's GPA may be used to represent the student's academic ability before coming to university. This is because data on students' pre-university academic performance cannot be traced – there is no national examination to include in the data every high school leaver's performance, and the first year GPA may be heavily influenced by the pre-university achievement. The third year's GPA is used to identify the academic progress during the undergraduate years. The third instead of the fourth year is used, due to a rather peculiar Japanese situation where many students manage to attain the necessary units to graduate by the end of third year to spend almost an entire fourth year for job search, so that their fourth year's GPAs do not reflect their academic ability.

(ii) Cooperative education: the total number of registrations for these courses is 5,132, with 1,190 in work-integrated learning (WIL) courses, which offer direct contacts with companies through internships, and 3,942 in inductive courses, which introduce to students various aspects of working life. In terms of student number, 1,789 took one cooperative education course and 1,275 took two or more, while 2,409 took none.

The basic statistics of the above data are summarized in Table 8-1.

It needs to be emphasized that cooperative education is not a well-established concept in Japan, as pointed out in Chapters 4 and 6 – according to the Ministry of Education, Culture, Science, Sports and Technology (see MEXT, 2013) on availability of internships, defined as programmes offering work experience, at universities as a part of cooperative education programme, the actual percentage of students participating in any internship is as low as 2.2 per cent of the entire body of university students, the duration of internship was less than mere 2 weeks in 61.6 per cent of the cases, and the students were reported to be paid for their work, transport, or meals only in 31 per cent of the universities who answered the questionnaires.

Table 8-1 Basic statistics (sample size = 5,160)

Variable name	Description	Mean	Median	Maximum	Minimum	Std. Dev.
(Cooperative education – CE)						
WIL	Dummy: 1 if at least one WIL taken	0.134	0.000	1.000	0.000	0.341
Induction	Dummy: if at least one Induction taken	0.433	0.000	1.000	0.000	0.496
NoCE	Number of CE courses taken	0.953	1.000	8.000	0.000	1.150
(Academic Performance)						
GPA		1.803	1.700	3.780	0.290	0.570
GPA1	Pre-university academic performance	1.896	1.910	3.760	0.000	0.684
GPA2		1.730	1.660	3.840	0.000	0.672
GPA3	University academic performance	1.896	1.830	4.000	0.000	0.689
GPA4		1.509	1.370	4.000	0.000	0.916
GradYr	Dummy: 1 if graduated in 2009 and 0 if in 2008	0.502	1.000	1.000	0.000	0.500
(Faculties)						
Economics	Dummy: 1 if Economics	0.237	0.000	1.000	0.000	0.425
Business	Dummy: 1 if Business	0.240	0.000	1.000	0.000	0.427
Law	Dummy: 1 if Law	0.220	0.000	1.000	0.000	0.414
Languages	Dummy: 1 if Languages	0.127	0.000	1.000	0.000	0.333
Cultural Studies	Dummy: 1 if Cultural Studies	0.082	0.000	1.000	0.000	0.274
Science	Dummy: 1 if Science	0.054	0.000	1.000	0.000	0.225
Engineering	Base group (does not appear in equation)	0.040	0.000	1.000	0.000	0.197
Gender	Dummy: 1 if male and 0 if female	0.706	1.000	1.000	0.000	0.456

(2) Estimated equation and variables

The equation estimated was Equation I of (7-1)"" with other variables related to the student's attributes:

$$CE = F (a1 + b1\ GPA1 + 11GradYr + m1\ Faculty + n1\ Gender) + u1\ (8\text{-}1)$$

where F represents a linear or non-linear form.

The variables used and the expected signs of coefficients are as follows:

(i) Dependent variable (CE): Three variables are used to quantify this variable

    a.   WIL: 1 if at least one cooperative education course is taken and 0 otherwise

    b.   Induction (Induction courses of cooperative education): 1 if at least one cooperative education course is taken and 0 otherwise

    c.   NoCE (A total number of cooperative education courses taken)

(ii) Independent variables

    a.   GPA1 (GPA in the first year)
       This is used in the place of PreU, since the latter is not available in Japan. The expected sign is positive if Hypothesis I holds.

    b.   GradYr (Year of graduation): 1 if the student graduates in 2009 and 0 if in 2008
       This variable attempts to detect if there is any tendency for taking cooperative education due to the year of graduation. At the same time including this variable makes other estimated coefficients independent of this effect. No sign is expected in advance.

    c.   Faculty (faculty the student belongs to): six dummies for seven faculties with Engineering Faculty being the reference category
       The term *faculty* in (8-1) has six terms and should be written in full as

$$m11E + m12B + m13J + m14L + m15C + m16S$$

       where E is Faculty of Economics, B is faculty of Business, J is faculty of Law, L is Faculty of Foreign Languages, C is Faculty of Cultural Studies, S is Faculty of Science, and Faculty of Engineering is the reference category.
       For example, a student of Faculty of Economics would have the dummy variables as: E = 1 and B, J, L, C, S = 0, while for a student of Faculty of Engineering E, B, J, L, C, S = 0
       No particular sign is expected in advance. If any coefficient appears as significant, it could be due to the curriculum policy or the characteristics of the student of that particular faculty. And if the university hopes to

offer cooperative education to students irrespective of faculty, some policy needs to be introduced to make all coefficients 0 such as more active promotion among student or coop firms for those faculties with negative coefficients.

d.   Gender: 1 if a student is male and 0 if female
There is no reason to expect cooperative education to be more popular among male or female students. But a policy of gender equality in opportunity may suggest to make this coefficient 0.

(3)   Estimation results

Equation I as in (8-1) was estimated with three different definitions of cooperative education as a dependent variable as explained above, that is, WIL, Induction and NoCE. Three qualitative response models – a linear probability model, a logit model, and a probit model, were used for estimation for the first two cases, where the dependent variables are 0/1 variables, and a linear model was used for the third case, where the dependent variable is quantitative. The estimation results are given below in turn.

(i)   Dependent variable: WIL – 1 if at least one cooperative education course is taken and 0 otherwise

The estimated equation is

$$\text{WIL} = F (a1 + b1 \text{ GPA1} + l1 \text{ GradYr} + m1 \text{ Faculty} + n1 \text{ Gender}) + u1 \tag{8-2}$$

where F follows a linear probability, a logit, or a probit model.

Table 8-2 shows the estimation results for the three models. A and B are both the estimation result of a linear probability model with ordinary least square (OLS) – the estimated coefficient are identical, but with different treatments of errors. As explained earlier, theoretically heteroskedasticity-robust t-values need to be used, because the error is not normally distributed, which also gives different set of standard errors and P-values. Note, however, the difference is rather small.

Comparing the four sets of results, that is, A, B, C, and D in Table 8-2, the signs and levels of significance of the estimated coefficients show similarities. Note, however, the coefficients for the same variables in the linear probability, logit, and probit models differ because of the way coefficients affects the dependent variable. The coefficients become comparable as "marginal effects" by multiplying them with a scale factor, which is either the average partial effect (APE) or the partial Effect at the average (PEA) to be calculated for logit and probit, or 0.25 and 0.4 for logit and probit respectively, as explained in Chapter 7. Table 8-3 shows the results of calculation. The marginal effects of the independent variables are calculated using three different scale factors, that is

Table 8-2 Estimation result

Dependent variable: WIL (sample size = 5,160)

A. Model: Linear probability, Method: OLS with heteroskedasticity-robust t-values (*)

Variable	Coefficient	Std. Error	t-value (*)	P-value
Constant	0.013	0.026484	0.493	0.622
GradYr	0.009	0.009277	0.994	0.320
Economics	0.016	0.019307	0.854	0.393
Business	0.074	0.020355	3.632	0.000
Law	0.049	0.020089	2.424	0.015
Languages	0.052	0.02317	2.261	0.024
Culture	0.100	0.026927	3.709	0.000
Science	0.036	0.026475	1.344	0.179
Gender	−0.077	0.012283	−6.279	0.000
GPA1	0.064	0.006876	9.337	0.000
Adjusted R²	0.043		F-statistic	27.022
			Prob (F-statistic)	0.000

B. Model: Linear probability, Method: OLS

Variable	Coefficient	Std. Error	t-value	P-value
Constant	0.013	0.029754	0.439	0.661
GradYr	0.009	0.00931	0.990	0.322
Economics	0.016	0.025015	0.659	0.510
Business	0.074	0.02502	2.955	0.003
Law	0.049	0.025201	1.932	0.053
Languages	0.052	0.027062	1.935	0.053
Culture	0.100	0.028737	3.475	0.001
Science	0.036	0.030693	1.160	0.246
Gender	−0.077	0.011483	−6.717	0.000
GPA1	0.064	0.007151	8.977	0.000
Adjusted R²	0.043		F-statistic	27.022
			Prob (F-statistic)	0

(Continued)

Table 8-2 (Continued)

C. Model: Logit, Method: ML

Variable	Coefficient	Std. Error	t-value	P-value
Constant	-3.358	0.325399	-10.319	0.000
GradYr	0.073	0.08412	0.870	0.384
Economics	0.238	0.28967	0.822	0.411
Business	0.795	0.28253	2.813	0.005
Law	0.598	0.287794	2.079	0.038
Languages	0.619	0.295061	2.097	0.036
Culture	0.962	0.300348	3.204	0.001
Science	0.467	0.327991	1.424	0.154
Gender	-0.584	0.095262	-6.128	0.000
GPA1	0.613	0.068231	8.977	0.000
McFadden R^2	0.057		LR statistic	232.718
			Prob(LR statistic)	0.000

D. Model: Probit, Method: ML

Variable	Coefficient	Std. Error	t-value	P-value
Constant	-1.8755	0.16376	-11.453	0.000
GradYr	0.0428	0.045452	0.941	0.347
Economics	0.1350	0.144228	0.936	0.349
Business	0.4207	0.141619	2.970	0.003
Law	0.3137	0.143787	2.182	0.029
Languages	0.3147	0.149338	2.108	0.035
Culture	0.5102	0.153406	3.326	0.001
Science	0.2461	0.166977	1.474	0.141
Gender	-0.3242	0.052826	-6.138	0.000
GPA1	0.3246	0.03639	8.921	0.000
McFadden R^2	0.057		LR statistic	230.853
			Prob(LR statistic)	0.000

(Note) Significant at 5%
        Significant at 10%

Table 8-3 Comparing the marginal effects

A. Scale factors (Rule of thumb: 0.25 for Logit and 0.4 for Probit)

Variable	Model: Linear probability		Model: Logit			Model: Probit		
	Coefficient	Marginal E	Coefficient	Marginal E	LP/Logit	Coefficient	Marginal E	LP/Probit
C	0.013	0.013	-3.358	-0.839	-0.016	-1.876	-0.750	-0.017
GradYr	0.009	0.009	0.073	0.018	0.504	0.043	0.017	0.539
E	0.016	0.016	0.238	0.060	0.277	0.135	0.054	0.305
B	0.074	0.074	0.795	0.199	0.372	0.421	0.168	0.439
J	0.049	0.049	0.598	0.150	0.326	0.314	0.125	0.388
L	0.052	0.052	0.619	0.155	0.339	0.315	0.126	0.416
C01	0.100	0.100	0.962	0.241	0.415	0.510	0.204	0.489
S	0.036	0.036	0.467	0.117	0.305	0.246	0.098	0.362
Gender	-0.077	-0.077	-0.584	-0.146	0.528	-0.324	-0.130	0.595
GPA1	0.064	0.064	0.613	0.153	0.419	0.325	0.130	0.494

B. Scale factors (APE: 0.111 for Logit and 0.204 for Probit)

Variable	Model: Linear probability		Model: Logit			Model: Probit		
	Coefficient	Marginal E	Coefficient	Marginal E	LP/Logit	Coefficient	Marginal E	LP/Probit
C	0.013	0.013	-3.358	-0.371	-0.035	-1.876	-0.383	-0.034
GradYr	0.009	0.009	0.073	0.008	1.139	0.043	0.009	1.056
E	0.016	0.016	0.238	0.026	0.626	0.135	0.028	0.598

(Continued)

Table 8-3 (Continued)

	Model: Linear probability		Model: Logit			Model: Probit		
Variable	Coefficient	Marginal E	Coefficient	Marginal E	LP/Logit	Coefficient	Marginal E	LP/Probit
B	0.074	0.074	0.795	0.088	0.841	0.421	0.086	0.860
J	0.049	0.049	0.598	0.066	0.736	0.314	0.064	0.760
L	0.052	0.052	0.619	0.068	0.766	0.315	0.064	0.815
C01	0.100	0.100	0.962	0.106	0.939	0.510	0.104	0.958
S	0.036	0.036	0.467	0.052	0.689	0.246	0.050	0.708
Gender	-0.077	-0.077	-0.584	-0.065	1.195	-0.324	-0.066	1.165
GPA1	0.064	0.064	0.613	0.068	0.948	0.325	0.066	0.968

C. Scale factors (PEA: 0.104 for Logit and 0.201 for Probit)

	Model: Linear probability		Model: Logit			Model: Probit		
Variable	Coefficient	Marginal E	Coefficient	Marginal E	LP/Logit	Coefficient	Marginal E	LP/Probit
C	0.013	0.013	-3.358	-0.350	-0.037	-1.876	-0.377	-0.035
GradYr	0.009	0.009	0.073	0.008	1.209	0.043	0.009	1.072
E	0.016	0.016	0.238	0.025	0.665	0.135	0.027	0.607
B	0.074	0.074	0.795	0.083	0.893	0.421	0.085	0.874
J	0.049	0.049	0.598	0.062	0.781	0.314	0.063	0.772
L	0.052	0.052	0.619	0.064	0.812	0.315	0.063	0.827
C01	0.100	0.100	0.962	0.100	0.996	0.510	0.103	0.973
S	0.036	0.036	0.467	0.049	0.731	0.246	0.049	0.719
SEX	-0.077	-0.077	-0.584	-0.061	1.268	-0.324	-0.065	1.183
GPA1	0.064	0.064	0.613	0.064	1.006	0.325	0.065	0.983

(A) the rule of thumb: 0.25 for logit and 0.4 for probit; (B) APE: 0.111 for logit and 0.204 for probit; and (C) PEA: 0.104 for logit and 0.201 for probit. The values are compared with the coefficients of the linear probability model in terms of the ratio in columns LP/Logit and LP/Probit. It can be seen that for APE and PEA the most of ratios are close to 1, meaning the coefficients of the linear probability model are close to those of the more theoretically rigorous models despite its theoretical defects. Thus one may sacrifice the theoretical rigour of logit and probit models for the simple and intuitive nature of linear probability models and the analysis below will be based on the OLS result, that is, A of Table 8-2.

Several points are worth mentioning. First, there is a faculty variation in the participation to cooperative education, with the estimated coefficient showing significance, that is, large t-values (roughly above 2 or below –2) or equivalently small P-values (below 0.1, 0.05, or 0.01), other than the faculties of economics and science. The positive and significant coefficients implies in these faculties students take cooperative education more often than those in the faculty of engineering, which is the reference category in the dummy setting. Note that the table shows "standard errors" for the estimated coefficients as well as the t-values and P-values. In fact, a t-value is calculated by dividing the estimated coefficient by the standard error, so that a usual table would have either standard errors or t-values. Second, the relative magnitudes among the faculties may be compared and the result shows for example that the estimated coefficient 0.1 for the faculty of cultural studies, which implies that those students have 10 per cent more probability of taking cooperative education courses than their engineering counterpart. Third, there was no difference in the year of graduation. Fourth, the gender difference is shown to be significant. The negative value in this setting implies that more female students are likely to take cooperative education courses by 7.7 per cent. Fifth, GPA1 shows a positive and significant causal relationship to the probability of taking cooperative education courses, which support Hypothesis I. Finally, adjusted R^2 is at about 4 per cent, which seems quite low. However, very low values of adjusted R^2 have been reported in binary response models. For example, Cox and Wermuth (1992) report of a case in which $R^2 = 0.124$ (R^2 is unadjusted R^2 which is lower than adjusted R^2), and yet, there is a clear causal relationship. The low adjusted R^2 also could mean some important variables were omitted, but this would not discredit the significance of certain variables, for the F-statistics in the equations negate the null hypothesis that all coefficients are zero, that is, Prob(F-value) is nearly 0 per cent in all equations.

What can the cooperative education organizers learn and suggest as policies to improve the programme from this result? There are at least three observations and policies relating to them. First, it is the faculty variation on the probability of students taking cooperative education courses. It should be pointed out that this variation is free from faculty characteristics such as male-female ratio or different GPA levels, for those elements are taken care of by the essence of multiple regression analysis. This was the issue not covered by the statistical approach in Chapter 6. If the university plans to popularize the cooperative education programme throughout all faculties, it should give more support to the Faculties of Economics and Science, whose coefficients are found to be not significantly different from zero, and Engineering, whose coefficient is zero by the definition of reference category. Or cooperative education may not be the right style of education for some disciplines in Japan, although it is more popular in science faculties than non-science faculties elsewhere. Second, male students are less likely to take cooperative education given faculty and GPA1 result. If the university wishes to provide equal opportunity for taking cooperative education to both male and female students, they should investigate the reason for the lower popularity among male students by means of, for example, student's questionnaires. Third, there seems to be a strong evidence that more academic competent students take cooperative education, which supports Hypothesis I. As suggested in the earlier chapter, this can cause to overestimate the effect of cooperative education on academic performance and employment outcomes. At the same time, more encouragement may be given to students with poorer academic performance in order to popularize the cooperative education programme at the university.

(ii)   Dependent variable: Induction – 1 if at least one induction course is taken and 0 otherwise

$$\text{Induction} = F\,(a1 + b1\ \text{GPA1} + l1\ \text{GradYr} + m1\ \text{Faculty}$$
$$+\ n1\ \text{Gender}) + u1 \tag{8-3}$$

where F follows a linear probability, a logit, or a probit model.

Only the dependent variable is different from (8-2). Here, it is whether at least one induction course is taken. The analogous estimation results appear in Table 8-4. Again, the estimation results do not differ greatly among four methods. Thus using A of Table 8-4 as before, that is, the result with heteroskedasticity-robust t-values, the main results may be summarized by the following four points. First, there were significantly higher probability of students taking induction courses in 2008 than in 2009. Second, as for the faculty variation, there is a significant differences among them, but the tendency is not exactly the same as for WIL above. Third, gender difference did not appear to exist. Finally, GPA1 was not affecting a probability of student taking any induction course and thus the estimation result with Induction as the dependent variable does not support Hypothesis I. The conclusion is that there is no particular characteristics of students who take induction courses except for faculty difference. One may suggest that some faculties, that is, law, cultural studies, science, and engineering, need to promote induction courses, to popularize the programme to all faculties equally.

Table 8-4 Estimation result

Dependent variable: Induction (sample size = 5,160)

A. Model: Linear probability, Method: OLS with heteroskedasticity-robust t-values (*)

Variable	Coefficient	Std. Error	t-value	P-value
Constant	0.418	0.043	9.740	0.000
GradYr	-0.091	0.014	-6.737	0.000
Economics	0.106	0.036	2.925	0.004
Business	0.149	0.036	4.105	0.000
Law	0.003	0.036	0.081	0.935
Languages	0.148	0.039	3.768	0.000
Culture	-0.071	0.041	-1.742	0.082
Science	-0.148	0.041	-3.586	0.000
Gender	-0.013	0.017	-0.771	0.441
GPA1	0.002	0.010	0.194	0.846
Adjusted R^2	0.039	F-statistic Prob (F-statistic)	24.336 0.000	

B. Model: Linear probability, Method: OLS

Variable	Coefficient	Std. Error	t-value	P-value
Constant	0.418	0.043	9.634	0.000
GradYr	-0.091	0.014	-6.743	0.000
Economics	0.106	0.036	2.901	0.004
Business	0.149	0.036	4.080	0.000
Law	0.003	0.037	0.080	0.936
Languages	0.148	0.039	3.761	0.000
Culture	-0.071	0.042	-1.694	0.090
Science	-0.148	0.045	-3.311	0.001
Gender	-0.013	0.017	-0.766	0.444
GPA1	0.002	0.010	0.194	0.846
Adjusted R^2	0.039	F-statistic Prob (F-statistic)	24.336 0	

(Continued)

Table 8-4 (Continued)

C. Model: Logit, Method: ML

Variable	Coefficient	Std. Error	t-value	P-value
Constant	-0.336	0.185	-1.814	0.070
GradYr	-0.386	0.058	-6.708	0.000
Economics	0.441	0.156	2.824	0.005
Business	0.614	0.156	3.936	0.000
Law	0.013	0.158	0.084	0.933
Languages	0.612	0.168	3.641	0.000
Culture	-0.318	0.183	-1.740	0.082
Science	-0.736	0.207	-3.560	0.000
Gender	-0.055	0.071	-0.769	0.442
GPA1	0.009	0.044	0.194	0.846
McFadden R^2	0.031	LR statistic	217.246	
		Prob (LR statistic)	0.000	

D. Model: Probit, Method: ML

Variable	Coefficient	Std. Error	t-value	P-value
Constant	-0.208	0.114	-1.819	0.069
GradYr	-0.240	0.036	-6.721	0.000
Economics	0.273	0.096	2.838	0.005
Business	0.382	0.096	3.972	0.000
Law	0.010	0.097	0.098	0.922
Languages	0.380	0.104	3.666	0.000
Culture	-0.194	0.112	-1.739	0.082
Science	-0.447	0.124	-3.613	0.000
Gender	-0.034	0.044	-0.776	0.438
GPA1	0.005	0.027	0.181	0.856
McFadden R^2	0.031	LR statistic	217.281	
		Prob (LR statistic)	0.000	

(Note) Significant at 5%
Significant at 10%

(iii) Dependent variable: NoCE – a total number of cooperative education related courses taken

$$NoCE = a1 + b1\ GPA1 + l1\ GradYr + m1\ Faculty$$
$$+ n1\ Gender + u1 \qquad (8\text{-}4)$$

The estimation result is shown in Table 8-5. As it is a simple linear model, only one equation is estimated with OLS with usual t-values and adjusted R^2. The main results may be summarized by five points. First, there is a significant difference in the year of graduation. Second, there is a faculty variation. It could be cause by some unknown student characteristics difference between the two groups or by the way the cooperative education was organised which differed in these two years. Further investigation would be necessary to find out the reason for the difference. Third, there is a gender difference. Female students seem to be keener to take cooperative education courses in general as well as WIL in (i). The coefficient of –0.285 implies that a male student on average takes 0.285 cooperative education courses less than the female counterpart. The same kind of investigation as in (i) may be necessary to have more

Table 8-5 Estimation result

Dependent variable: NoCE (sample size = 5,160)

Model: Linear, Method: OLS

Variable	Coefficient	Std. Error	t-value	P-value
Constant	0.618	0.099	6.250	0.000
GradYr	–0.143	0.031	–4.623	0.000
Economics	0.247	0.083	2.966	0.003
Business	0.545	0.083	6.549	0.000
Law	0.186	0.084	2.225	0.026
Languages	0.603	0.090	6.707	0.000
Culture	0.049	0.096	0.516	0.606
Science	–0.123	0.102	–1.204	0.229
Gender	–0.285	0.038	–7.466	0.000
GPA1	0.160	0.024	6.725	0.000
Adjusted R^2	0.071			
F-statistic	45.135			
Prob(F-statistic)	0.000			
(Note)		Significant at 5%		
		Significant at 10%		

male students taking cooperative education courses. Fourth, the students with higher GPA1 tend to take more cooperative education courses as well as WIL, which support Hypothesis I. Again, by the same argument as for WIL, this can cause the effect of cooperative education on GPA3 to be overestimated. And fifth, adjusted R^2 is low as in (i) and (ii), and yet this is not a binary response model. One possible cause is that the dependent variable did not vary greatly. This can be detected by Table 8-1, in which NoCE varies from 0 to 8, but its median was 1 and mean was 0.953. It seems that most of the values were either 0 or 1, making the dependent variable almost as a binary response and thus giving a low adjusted R^2.

This chapter has shown how econometric methods can be used on available data for cooperative education, to identify the background for students taking cooperative education courses. A linear causal relationship was estimated using a simple least square method when a dependent variable, that is, the number of cooperative education courses, takes a positive value, while non-linear relationship was added when a dependent variable takes a binary response, that is, whether at least one WIL is taken and whether at least one induction courses is taken. In the binary response case, a linear probability model, a logit model, and a probit model were used for estimation and the coefficients were compared. A linear probability model is less theoretically rigorous but simpler to use and more intuitive than the other two. Furthermore, the estimated coefficients do not differ greatly from those of the logit and probit models.

The estimated results of the linear probability models based on OLS show several features among the students who take cooperative education courses. First, there is a faculty variation. It may be due to the nature of the discipline or the way the faculty introduces cooperative education course to the students. But if the university aims to popularize cooperative education to all faculties, then a pinpoint policy on faculty may be needed. Second, gender plays an important role in deciding to take cooperative education courses in general and WIL in particular – female students are keener that male counterparts. It may be needed to make male students more aware of and accessible to cooperative education. Third, pre-university academic performance expressed by GPA1 was a significant determining factor for taking cooperative education courses in general and WIL in particular, thereby supporting Hypothesis I. The implication of this result is that even if cooperative education shows a positive effect on academic performance at university or employment outcomes – these are the topics of Chapters 9 and 10, it may not be the sole cause – those well-to-do students were not merely the products of cooperative education but came to the programme already as a well-to-do students to some extent.

The next chapter deals with the causes of high academic performance at university by estimation Equation II, where cooperative education is considered as the cause alongside pre-university academic performance. In so doing, an international comparison is made based on KSU data and data from Honk Kong Polytechnic University.

9 Does cooperative education programme help raise academic performance in Japan and in Hong Kong?

This chapter shows how to verify the effect of cooperative education on academic performance by estimating:

Equation II: Acad = a2 + b2 PreU + c2 CE + u2   (9-1)

More specifically, the interest lies in testing the following two hypotheses:

Hypothesis V: Cooperative education affects academic performance at university.
Hypothesis III: Pre-university academic performance affects academic performance at university.

It is crucial for the advocates and practitioners of cooperative education to show that Hypothesis V holds in a positive way, that is, cooperative education raises academic performance at university, in order to obtain support for their programme from other academic and administrative members of the university. It needs to be shown that cooperative education compliments rather than substitutes other academic programmes. By contrast, for all engaged in university education, a positive causality in Hypothesis III could undermine the value of university education itself – if academic performance is largely predetermined by pre-university academic performance, what is the value of university education? The discussion will be extended to include an international comparison between two universities – Kyoto Sangyo University (KSU) of Japan and Hong Kong Polytechnic University (PolyU) of Hong Kong. The content of this chapter is largely based on Tanaka (2012) and Tanaka and Carlson (2012).

(1) A regression analysis of KSU data

As in the estimation of Equation I, the variable CE is defined by work-integrated learning (WIL), Induction, and NoCE, and the following four equations were estimated:

$$GPA3 = a2 + b2\ GPA1 + c2WIL + l2GradYr + m2Faculty$$
$$+ n2Gender + u2 \tag{9-2}$$

$$GPA3 = a2 + b2\ GPA1 + c2Induction + l2GradYr + m2Faculty$$
$$+ n2Gender + u2 \tag{9-3}$$

$$GPA3 = a2 + b2\ GPA1 + c2NoCE + l2GradYr + m2Faculty$$
$$+ n2Gender + u2 \tag{9-4}$$

$$GPA3 = a2 + b2\ GPA1 + c21WIL + c22Induction + l2GradYr$$
$$+ m2Faculty + n2Gender + u2 \tag{9-5}$$

where GPA3 replaces Acad, and GPA1 replaces PreU in (9-1), and a set of personal attributes, that is, GradYr, Faculty, and Gender are included as in Equation I of Chapter 8.

Note that (9-5) has two variables for CE. This is because WIL and Induction may have different effects on GPA3, as the former is more advanced than the latter. The main concerns here are whether the academic performance at university is influenced by cooperative education (i.e. Hypothesis V, or equivalently $c2 \neq 0$) and pre-university academic performance (i.e. Hypothesis III, or equivalently $b2 \neq 0$).

The same set of KSU data as in Chapter 7 was used, and Table 9-1 shows the estimation results of regressing GPA3 on GPA1 and cooperative education variables as well as other personal attributes of the students. Four equations were estimated with a variation in the cooperative education as an independent variables. It is a common empirical procedure in econometrics to run a set of regressions with partly different independent variables depending on the definition of the variable. All equations show the same signs and the significance for all variables except for cooperative education variables as well as reasonable level of adjusted R^2 around 0.4. Equation 1, 2, and 3 use NoCE, WIL, and Induction respectively as a CE variable, while Equation 4 uses WIL and Induction for CE.

In all equations, GradYr show negative and significant coefficients, implying that graduates of 2009 had lower GPA3 than the 2008 counterparts, or the 2009 graduates were less academically competent than the 2008 counterparts – this is a plausible hypothesis as the general academic level seems to continue falling in Japan but further investigation in this issue needs to be made elsewhere. The faculty coefficients, Faculty, show a more worrying tendency. For example, the gap between students in faculties of culture and economics in Equation 1 is $0.229 - (-0.105) = 0.334$, which is a considerable size for GPA. This is either or both because of inter-faculty difference in students' academic standard or in marking criterion. It is an important issue but also outside of the scope of the present research. Male students seem to perform worse academically as the coefficients are all negative and significant.

The estimate for GPA1 is very important for our purpose. It says a higher GPA1 causes a higher GPA3 and the relationship is significant. More specifically, 1-point rise in GPA1 generates just below 0.6-point rise in GPA3 in all four equations. This supports "Hypothesis III: Pre-university academic performance

Linear model estimated by ordinary least square method

Equation	1		2		3		4	
Dependent variable: GPA3 (sample size = 5,160)								
	Coefficient	t-value	Coefficient	t-value	Coefficient	t-value	Coefficient	t-value
Constant	0.856	17.851	0.858	18.018	0.878	18.232	0.865	17.974
Grad in 2009	−0.046	−3.093	−0.048	−3.242	−0.051	−3.415	−0.050	−3.323
Economics	−0.105	−2.624	−0.106	−2.641	−0.099	−2.472	−0.104	−2.591
Business	−0.016	−0.395	−0.021	−0.524	−0.006	−0.147	−0.018	−0.446
Law	0.037	−0.905	0.032	0.796	0.038	0.939	0.033	0.808
Languages	0.126	0.885	0.124	2.854	0.136	3.135	0.127	2.914
Culture	0.229	4.953	0.217	4.713	0.226	4.895	0.217	4.706
Science	−0.058	−1.174	−0.063	−1.278	−0.065	−1.320	−0.065	−1.320
Gender	−0.108	−5.838	−0.101	−5.470	−0.111	−6.005	−0.102	−5.511
GPA1	0.592	51.328	0.585	50.725	0.593	51.687	0.586	50.711
Career NoCE	0.007	0.975						
WIL			0.117	5.259			0.109	4.544
Induction					−0.043	−2.828	−0.017	−1.006
Adjusted R²	0.398		0.400		0.398		0.400	
F-statistic	340.212		344.647		341.381		313.408	
Pro (F-statistic)	0		0		0		0	
					(Note)		Significant at 5%	
							Significant at 10%	

affects academic performance" in a positive manner or "Good high school leavers make good university students," but not to a full extent, leaving a considerable room for hard work at university.

Finally, the cooperative education coefficients show mixed results. NoCE or a number of cooperative education courses has no notable effect on GPA3 in Equation 1, while WIL is positive and significant in Equations 2 and 3. The effect of Induction is negative but significant only when it appears without WIL. One can conclude that what is academically effective is work-integrated learning programmes where teaching is intensive, while Induction courses may be attended as remedial courses by students with low GPA, giving negative coefficients. One may conclude that CE defined by WIL supports "Hypothesis V: Cooperative education affects academic performance at university" in a positive manner or "Cooperative education helps students academically."

(2)   A regression analysis to compare KSU and PolyU

PolyU and its cooperative education programme

Throughout its history, the PolyU has been an application-oriented educational institution. Prior to attaining full university status in 1994, it was both a Polytechnic and even longer in its history a Technical College. PolyU is a large government-funded tertiary institution in Hong Kong with a total of 28,000 students (about 15,000 in government-funded programmes). Given this history, WIL has a long record at PolyU in those programmes where professional qualifications and licensure are required. However, this history is not pervasive across all students and programmes. In the 2005/6 Academic Year, PolyU admitted its first cohort that was subject to a compulsory WIL requirement for government-funded undergraduate degrees. Each student under this requirement must have at least one WIL placement at least equivalent to two full working weeks (e.g. 80 hours). PolyU has six faculties and two schools – Faculty of Applied Science and Textiles, Faculty of Business, Faculty of Construction and Land Use, Faculty of Engineering, Faculty of Humanities, Faculty of Health and Social Science, School of Hotel and Tourism Management, and School of Design.

PolyU data

A total of 1,373 undergraduate students were included in this study (58.8 per cent male, 41.2 per cent female). Only students who had complete data were included: these included an online survey, as well as complete university records for their first and third year GPA. PolyU currently employs a 3-year undergraduate curriculum. Average GPAs for the first and third years were 2.96 and 3.16 respectively. Three variables were collected via an online exit survey on WIL: number of WIL placements completed, learning outcomes from WIL, and perceived working context. All other variables were collected via a centralized university unit responsible for maintaining student academic records.

An invitation to complete the online survey was emailed to all eligible students (i.e. those required to complete WIL for their undergraduate degree). The only incentive given to the students was a WIL transcript providing relevant details for use in future job applications. The overall response rate was 45.5 per cent, which is fairly good for an institution-wide voluntary survey. The response rates varied by faculty/school affiliation – ranging from 14.4 per cent to 57.3 per cent, although five of the eight faculties/schools had response rates above 50 per cent. Those faculties/schools with the lowest response rates were possibly caused by students not being motivated by the WIL transcript as they had other forms of documentation more valued by prospective employers (e.g., centralized records related to professional practice and qualification, professional portfolio). For many of these students, their WILs would have been well-structured and supervised – hence this sampling may have missed some of the higher quality WIL experiences. In addition, it was believed that students with lower-quality WILs would also lack motivation to obtain a WIL transcript, as they would not be useful to gain employment. However, there was no way to substantiate this last claim.

As explained earlier, WIL is mandatory in PolyU; thus, its effect on academic performance cannot be determined with one/zero dummy variable. In order to express the WIL experience of each student, three variables were used: Number of Placements, Overall Learning Outcomes, and Overall Learning Context. Number of Placements simply refers to the number of WIL placements a student completed during their undergraduate studies. While the range was very large (1–18), the average was 2.01 per student with a large majority completing one or two.

Learning outcomes during their WIL experiences were rated by each student on a 10-point scale – using 14 specific outcome items and one overall rating. These items covered such areas as initiative, responsibility, communication and teamwork skills, problem solving, systematic thinking, applying academic knowledge to the real world, and a better understanding of the workplace environment. A 10-point scale was chosen for the learning outcomes as students are very familiar with having their learning rated on such a scale at the university. The variable Overall Learning Outcomes is derived by aggregating student ratings across all of these items. The range for this variable is large (15–150), with an average of 108.29.

Students also rated their perceived working context on 10 items on a 6-point scale. These items included questions about the quantity and quality of workplace feedback, self-motivation (efforts to learn things in their WIL), and interest and challenge of job tasks. A 6-point scale was chosen as being able to meaningfully differentiate student experiences. The questionnaire assessing the learning outcomes and learning context was piloted during a summer program (1,053 students) and was found to be a useful index of student experiences. The variable Overall Learning Context is derived by aggregating student ratings across all of these items. The range for this variable is 10–60, with an average of 44.06. The above figures are shown together with KSU figures, which is modified to include 2010 data to compare with PolyU's 2010 data in Table 9-2.

Table 9-2 Basic statistics for KSU and PolyU

University	KSU				PolyU
Graduating year	2008	2009	2010		2010
No. of students	2,572	2,588	2,478		1,373 (sampled)
Male	1,847	1,794	1,747		807
Female	725	794	731		566
Average 1st yr GPA	1.86	1.94	1.8		2.96
Average 3rd yr GPA	1.89	1.9	1.91		3.16
No. of students with				Average no. of	
At least one CE* course	1,555	1,216	1,705	WIL placements	2.01
WIL	325	367	298	Average rating of	
Induction	1,230	1,005	1,477	OLO**	108.29
				OLC***	44.06

(*) CE: Cooperative education = WIL *and* Induction course
(**) OLO: Overall Learning Outcomes
(***) OLC: Overall Learning Context

Estimation results for KSU and PolyU

A multiple regression analysis was employed to estimate the effects of WIL and pre-university grade on final year GPA using OLS method. The actual variables used were the third year GPA (GPA3) as the dependent variable and WIL, the first year GPA (GPA1), student gender (Gender), and faculty/school affiliation (Faculty) as the independent variables. For KSU, WIL was indexed via two variables: WIL participation (1 if yes and 0 otherwise), and induction course participation (1 if yes and 0 otherwise). For PolyU, the effects of WIL were indexed via the three variables described earlier: Number of Placements (No. of WIL), Overall Learning Outcomes (OLO), and Overall Learning Context (OLC). Therefore, the equations estimated are for KSU:

$$\text{GPA3} = \text{Constant} + b_1 \text{ WIL} + b_2 \text{ Induction} + b_4 \text{ GPA1} + b_5 \text{ Gender} + b_6 \text{ Faculty} + u \tag{9-6}$$

and for PolyU:

$$\text{GPA3} = \text{Constant} + b_1 \text{ No. of WIL} + b_2 \text{ OLO} + b_3 \text{ OLC} + b_4 \text{ GPA1} + b_5 \text{ Gender} + b_6 \text{ Faculty} + u \tag{9-7}$$

where Constant and b's are the coefficients to be estimated and the terms are the variables.

Table 9-3 Regression result on KSU data

Estimated equation:

$$Y = C + b_1X_1 + b_2X_2 + b_4X_4 + b_5X_5 + b_{61}X_{61} + b_{62}X_{62} + b_{63}X_{63} + b_{64}X_{64} + b_{65}X_{65} + b_{66}X_{66}$$

Dependent variable (Y): GPA3

	2008		2009		2010	
Independent var.	*Coefficient*	*P-value*	*Coefficient*	*P-value*	*Coefficient*	*P-value*
WIL (X_1) (D)	.119**	0.001	.104**	0	0.038	0.33
Induction (X_2) (D)	0.005	0.826	−0.027	0.25	0.01	0.954
1st year GPA (X_4)	.548**	0	.620**	0	582**	0
Gender (X_5) (D)	−.105**	0	−.096**	0	−.093**	0.001
Economics (X_{61}) (D)	−0.08	0.175	−.126*	0.021	−.151**	0.01
Business (X_{62}) (D)	0.002	0.977	−0.035	0.525	0.087	0.127
Law (X_{63}) (D)	0.11	0.066	−0.033	0.548	−0.049	0.394
Languages (X_{64}) (D)	0.102	0.11	.149*	0.012	0.112	0.071
Cultures (X_{65}) (D)	.270**	0	.163*	0.011	−0.045	0.5
Science (X_{66}) (D)	0.03	0.673	−.151*	0.025	−.172*	0.016
Constant (C)	0.893		0.779		0.947	
Adjusted R^2 =	0.365		0.436		0.398	
Sample size	2,572		2,588		2,478	

Note: **: p < .01; *: p < .05, D: Dummy variable

The results for KSU in 2008, 2009, and 2010 and PolyU in 2010 are displayed in Table 9-3 and Table 9-4 respectively. Overall, the models work fairly well in estimating the equations, with KSU's adjusted R^2 ranging from .365 to .436 and PolyU's being .402. The estimated coefficients b's are marked with a single asterisk if they are significant at 5 per cent level and with double asterisks if they are significant at 1 per cent level. For both institutions, WIL did show some effects. For KSU, the 2010 graduates showed no significant effects of WIL, while for the 2008 and 2009 graduates, WIL participation was shown to be related to higher third year GPA, both with a statistically significant level. Induction courses at KSU did not show a significant effect on the third year GPA.

For PolyU, the number of placements completed and overall learning context were not significant predictors. However, Overall Learning Outcomes was shown to be associated with higher third-year GPA with a statistical significance. While these effects were quite modest, they show promise in terms of various ways to index the WIL experience and its possible effects.

Table 9-4 PolyU regression results: 2010 graduates

Estimated equation:

$$Y = C + b_1X_1 + b_2X_2 + b_3X_3 + b_4X_4 + b_5X_5 + b_{61}X_{61} + b_{62}X_{62} + b_{63}X_{63} + b_{64}X_{64} + b_{65}X_{65} + b_{66}X_{66}$$

Dependent variable (Y): 3rd year GPA

Independent variable	Coefficient	P-value
Number of WIL Placements (X1)	−0.008	0.178
Overall Learning Outcomes (X2)	.002*	0.016
Overall Learning Context (X3)	−0.003	0.104
1st year GPA (X4)	.574**	0
Gender (X5) (D)	−.050*	0.017
Applied Science & Textiles (X61) (D)	−0.07	0.369
Business (X62) (D)	0.017	0.822
Construction & Land Use (X63) (D)	.156*	0.052
Engineering (X64) (D)	0.014	0.851
Humanities (X65) (D)	−0.061	0.471
Health & Social Science (X66) (D)	0.036	0.667
Hotel & Tourism Management (X67) (D)	0	0.992
Design (Basic group)		
Constant (C)	1.444	
Adjusted R²	0.402	
Sample size	1,373	

Note: **: $p < .01$; *: $p < .05$, D: Dummy variable

For both institutions, first-year GPA was a substantial predictor of third-year GPA. While this finding is not surprising in general, it is surprising that in both cases and across different cohorts in KSU, the weight of this predictor is somewhere between 0.5 and 0.6. Thus, first-year GPA contributes as much as a half of third-year GPA. Furthermore, at both institutions, females outperformed their male counterparts in their third-year GPA. This result was statistically significant in both institutions with the effect being more pronounced in Japan. Namely, a KSU female student does better than her male counterpart by about 0.1 GPA in the third year, while the figure reduces to 0.05 in PolyU.

For PolyU, there was only one small effect of faculty/school membership. However, these effects seemed more pronounced at KSU. The possible explanation is either that the general academic standard of students varies or the grading standard varies among faculties. It is difficult at this stage to pinpoint the reason without further investigation. At PolyU, exams and grading are well monitored and hence may be more standardized than at many other universities worldwide.

Conclusion

This investigation attempted to compare WIL programmes of different countries, probably one of the first attempts to do such evaluative international comparisons of WIL. Even when only two countries, such as Japan and Hong Kong, are compared, there are problems to solve in order to make it a meaningful comparison. For example, what can be used to measure the pre-university academic ability? Or, how can WILs of different formats be compared? In this sense, this chapter's treatment is far from the ideal. Yet there is no doubt that the benefit of such an attempt clearly outweighs the problems, especially for the practitioners and advocates of WIL programmes who hope to spread the concept globally.

With respect to the comparisons made in the investigation, several interesting results arose. First, Hypothesis V was "partially" supported. In Japan, the three graduating cohorts showed a positive effect of WIL on third year GPA, with two being significant, that is, 2008 and 2009. As for the non-significant result of 2010, the investigation needs to be continued for at least a few more years to verify whether this was a mere temporary outcome or a reflection of declining effect of WIL at KSU.

The Hong Kong sample also "partially" supported Hypothesis V – in that one of the three variables measuring individual differences in the WIL experience was significantly related to third year GPA. The number of WIL placements not being related to third year GPA is not surprising in that this is more a sheer number count that is not necessarily related to the actual quality of the placements. The individual differences in the quality of WIL were indexed by student-reported learning outcomes as well as the learning context. Only the overall learning outcomes variable was found to be significantly related to higher third year GPA. It is possible that the overall learning context variable functioned as a suppressor variable in the regression.

Overall learning outcomes being related to subsequent academic performance suggests possible linkages of what is learned in WIL back to the academic programme of the student. Often, this linkage has been discussed in terms of generic, soft skills related to organizational and study skills. However, this discussion surprisingly neglects the possibility of enhanced conceptual understanding from tackling problems in the real-world. Of course, this type of linkage would be stronger in placements related to the student's academic discipline. At PolyU, this type of data concerning the extent of placements being related to a student's discipline is now being collected, and this issue can be further examined. In terms of the present data, some simple post hoc correlational item-level analyses were conducted and the top three item level correlations suggest both processes may affect subsequent academic performance. Two items of more a generic nature (developing initiative in the WIL, and gaining a better understanding of the workplace) were in the top three item level correlations with third year GPA. Furthermore, the item specifically querying improving the student's ability to apply theories and concepts learned at the university in the real world was also substantially related to subsequent academic performance. Investigating these workplace learning processes and their impact on academic development is a fruitful area of future research, especially since this may have implications for placement selection and approval by universities.

Second, Hypothesis III was supported both in Japan and Hong Kong, with very similar estimated values of around 0.5 ~ 0.6 in both institutions, suggesting that first-year GPA contributes to about a half of third-year GPA. It would be interesting to see if this value holds for other countries.

Third, it is also worth noting that female students were observed to outperform their male counterparts in both KSU and PolyU. Again, it would be interesting to verify this in other countries. While there are many studies on gender differences in pre-university achievement and in terms of differential patterns of cognitive achievement, there is a surprisingly little amount of research literature on gender differences in overall university GPA (Conger and Long, 2010). A recent analysis by Conger and Long examining 16 American universities (from Florida and Texas) found that female university students had higher GPAs in their first semester versus their male counterparts. Furthermore, this gap widened as these students continued their undergraduate studies. While these authors did not measure this variable directly, they partially explained this gap based upon previous research on gender differences in pre-university achievement suggesting that non-cognitive abilities (e.g. self-discipline, organization, dependability) promoted these differences (Duckworth and Seligman, 2006).

Finally, the theoretical framework and methodology employed in this chapter were based on those often used by economists. But this by no means implies an exclusion of approaches of other disciplines such as psychology and sociology. It is hoped that eventually a standard approach will be developed with which the practitioners and advocates of WIL from different disciplines can collaborate globally.

10 Does cooperative education have positive effects on job search and job performance?

This chapter shows how to verify the effects of cooperative education on job search and performance by estimation Equation III: $Emp = a_3 + b_3 PreU + c_3 CE + d_3 Acad + u_3$. And in particular, the interest lies in testing the following hypotheses:

Hypothesis II: Pre-university academic performance affects employment outcome.

Hypothesis IV: Cooperative education affects employment outcome.

Hypothesis VI: Academic performance at university affects employment outcome.

Two types of employment outcome are considered for the investigation of the Japanese case. The first is the category of the first job after graduation – each student is asked whether the job is a full-time job or a part-time job and whether the job offering company is listed or unlisted. In both cases, the former, that is, a full-time job or a listed company, is generally considered to be a better choice than the latter, that is, a part-time job or an unlisted company. This is largely due to the Japanese labour market practice described by lifetime employment and wage seniority, which provides stability and security, and is more notable in full-time jobs than in part-time jobs and in large companies than in small companies. Consequently, in a country where lifetime employment and seniority wage is not common, the quality of employment may have to be defined differently. Another peculiarity of the Japanese labour market is that for graduates, a job search starts while they are still studying and most of them would have confirmed job offers before graduation. This makes it possible for the universities to obtain the data on job type and company status from all students before graduation. In a more usual situation where a student starts a job search after graduation, the data collection might have to be conducted by mail or telephone questionnaires with a less than full response rate.

The second type is how job is perceived by the Kyoto Sangyo University (KSU) alumni – those who graduated between 2006 and 2009 KSU were asked about their job satisfaction, skill formation, and work attitudes. The response of each alumni was matched with his or her attributes as a student such as graduation year, faculty, gender, and GPAs. Unlike the student data, which was available from every student, the response rate was much lower at 13 per cent. But this investigation can connect one's academic life at university and working life at company more profoundly as the questions are about how the alumni feel at work. In both investigations, the Hypotheses II, IV, and VI were tested, using the binary response model employed in earlier chapters. Below, these two types of approaches are discussed in turn. The data analysis and the discussion in this chapter are partly based on Tanaka (2012).

(1) Does cooperative education have positive effects on job search?

The data collected for 2008 and 2009 graduates, which are partly used in Chapters 8 and 9, include data on job status and company status of student's first job after graduation. While for the estimation of Equations I in Chapter 8 and Equation II in Chapter 9 the sample size is 5,160, the valid sample sizes for job status, that is, full-time or part-time, and company status, that is, listed or unlisted, are 4,616 and 3,965 respectively. Those who opted for graduate school and other further studies and those who found employment in public sectors are excluded from these figures. The basic statistics for the two sample sets are shown in Table 10-1A and B. Note that most of students find full-time jobs upon graduation (i.e. 90.9 per cent), while about one in three (i.e. 34.1 per cent) finds a post in a listed company.

Equation III: Emp = F (a3 + b3 PreU + c3 CE + d3 Acad) + u3, is estimated with a binary dependent variable FT (1 if it is a full-time job and 0 if it is a part-time job) or Listed (1 if it is a listed company and 0 if it is an unlisted company). Furthermore, as in Chapters 8 and 9, GPA1 and GPA3 replace PreU and Acad respectively with additional personal attributes such as GradYr, Faculty, and Gender. Thus Equation III to be estimated is

$$FT = F (a3 + b3 \text{ GPA3} + c3 \text{ CE} + d3 \text{ GPA1} + 13 \text{ GradYr} + m3 \text{ Faculty} + n3 \text{ Gender}) + u3 \qquad (10\text{-}1)$$

or

$$\text{Listed} = F (a3 + b3 \text{ GPA3} + c3 \text{ CE} + d3 \text{ GPA1} + 13 \text{ GradYr} + m3 \text{ Faculty} + n3 \text{ Gender}) + u3 \qquad (10\text{-}2)$$

In both cases, Hypothesis IV is tested with c3 = 0, Hypothesis II is tested with d3 = 0, and Hypothesis VI is tested with b3 = 0. If these coefficients are estimated to be non-zero with significance, then these hypotheses hold – one would expect the signs to be positive than negative to ensure that education contributes to employment, be it pre-university (Hypothesis II), university (Hypothesis VI), or cooperative (Hypothesis IV).

Table 10-1A Basic statistics for full-time and part-time category (sample size = 4,616)

Variable name	Description	Mean	Median	Maximum	Minimum	Std. Dev.
(Job status)						
FT	Dummy: 1 if full-time and 0 if part-time	0.909	1.000	1.000	0.000	0.288
(Cooperative education – CE)						
WIL	Dummy: 1if at least one WIL taken	0.139	0.000	1.000	0.000	0.346
Induction	Dummy: if at least one Induction taken	0.446	0.000	1.000	0.000	0.497
NoCE	Number of CE courses taken	0.983	1.000	8.000	0.000	1.153
(Academic Performance)						
GPA		1.799	1.700	3.710	0.290	0.566
GPA1	Pre-university academic performance	1.897	1.920	3.760	0.000	0.683
GPA2		1.729	1.660	3.840	0.000	0.669
GPA3	University academic performance	1.894	1.830	4.000	0.000	0.686
GPA4		1.482	1.350	4.000	0.000	0.904
GradYr	Dummy: 1 if graduated in 2009 and 0 if in 2008	0.497	0.000	1.000	0.000	0.500
(Faculty)						
Economics	Dummy: 1 if Economics	0.243	0.000	1.000	0.000	0.429
Business	Dummy: 1 if Business	0.251	0.000	1.000	0.000	0.434
Law	Dummy: 1 if Law	0.207	0.000	1.000	0.000	0.405
Languages	Dummy: 1 if Languages	0.131	0.000	1.000	0.000	0.337
Cultural Studies	Dummy: 1 if Cultural Studies	0.086	0.000	1.000	0.000	0.281
Science	Dummy: 1 if Science	0.048	0.000	1.000	0.000	0.214
Engineering	Reference category (does not appear in equation)	0.034	0.000	1.000	0.000	0.182
Gender	Dummy: 1 if male and 0 if female	0.699	1.000	1.000	0.000	0.459

Table 10-1B Basic statistics for listed and unlisted category (sample size = 3,965)

Variable name	Description	Mean	Median	Maximum	Minimum	Std. Dev.
Listed	Dummy: 1 if listed and 0 if unlisted	0.341	0.000	1.000	0.000	0.474
(Cooperative education – CE)						
WIL	Dummy: 1if at least one WIL taken	0.150	0.000	1.000	0.000	0.357
INDUCTION	Dummy: if at least one Induction taken	0.459	0.000	1.000	0.000	0.498
NoCE	Number of CE courses taken	1.031	1.000	8.000	0.000	1.172
(Academic Performance)						
GPA		1.820	1.720	3.710	0.470	0.558
GPA1	Pre-university academic performance	1.928	1.950	3.760	0.000	0.670
GPA2		1.748	1.690	3.840	0.000	0.661
GPA3	University academic performance	1.919	1.850	4.000	0.000	0.672
GPA4		1.492	1.360	4.000	0.000	0.910
GradYr	Dummy: 1 if graduated in 2009 and 0 if in 2008	0.490	0.000	1.000	0.000	0.500
(Faculty)						
Economics	Dummy: 1 if Economics	0.250	0.000	1.000	0.000	0.433
Business	Dummy: 1 if Business	0.263	0.000	1.000	0.000	0.440
Law	Dummy: 1 if Law	0.191	0.000	1.000	0.000	0.393
Languages	Dummy: 1 if Languages	0.131	0.000	1.000	0.000	0.337
Cultural Studies	Dummy: 1 if Cultural Studies	0.085	0.000	1.000	0.000	0.279
Science	Dummy: 1 if Science	0.043	0.000	1.000	0.000	0.204
Engineering	Reference category (does not appear in equation)	0.037	0.000	1.000	0.000	0.189
Gender	Dummy: 1 if male and 0 if female	0.690	1.000	1.000	0.000	0.462

This is a binary response model, and thus both equations (10-1) and (10-2) can be estimated by a linear probability model with ordinary least square (OLS) or by a logit or a probit model with Maximum Likelihood Estimation (MLE). Here, a linear probability model is employed for estimation with OLS, based on the discussions in Chapter 6 that a linear probability model is simple and intuitive and in Chapter 8 that the actual estimated values do not diverge greatly from the more theoretically rigorous logit or probit models although it misses some theoretical rigour of econometric reasoning.

Therefore, the estimated equations are:

$$FT = a3 + b3 \ GPA3 + c3 \ CE + d3 \ GPA1 + l3 \ GradYr$$
$$+ m3 \ Faculty + n3 \ Gender + u3 \qquad (10\text{-}1)'$$
$$Listed = a3 + b3 \ GPA3 + c3 \ CE + d3 \ GPA1 + l3 \ GradYr$$
$$+ m3 \ Faculty + n3 \ Gender + u3 \qquad (10\text{-}2)'$$

Table 10-2A shows the estimation result with employment status as a dependent variable and a set of independent variables appear along the first column. Four equations are estimated with a variation in the definition of cooperative education, that is, NoCE, WIL, Induction, and WIL and Induction. Several observations are worth noting. First, adjusted R^2 values for the fitness of the model are around 3 per cent. But as it was explained in Chapter 8, it does not negate the whole approach, although there may be some other important independent variables to consider. In any case, F-values and the near 0 per cent of Prob(F statistics), which means the probability of null hypothesis that all the coefficients are zero, support the validity of the estimation results as a whole.

As for the coefficients, most of them show t-values to imply significance at 5 per cent, apart from the faculty difference for Economics, Business, and Law. The year of graduation seems to matter – in Equation 1, for example, if you graduate in 2009, your probability of obtaining a full-time employment is 1.9 per cent below those in 2008. This could well be the consequence of the Lehman shock. The faculty difference seems to exist between engineering students and others with engineering students performing better than all others, as the coefficients are all negative, although the results are significant only for Languages, Cultural Studies, or Science students. It may suggest that engineering students have a better employment prospect. Gender seems to affect the employment prospect with being a male student significantly raising the probability of obtaining a full-time job by 2.2~2.5 per cent in equations 1~4. It is interesting to compare this with the earlier result that female students doing better at studies – so female students do better at university but worse for job search. This result was somehow expected with the existence of what is termed as a *statistical discrimination* against female candidates in the graduate labour market in Japan. In this context, the discrimination refers to the company's preference of a male candidate to a female candidate for a full-time post, because the latter is more likely to quit for marriage, child birth, or child bearing, thereby preventing the employer from getting returns from on-the-job training human capital investment. And it is "statistical" because the decision of the employer not to employ

Table 10-2A Determining factors of employment outcome by employment status

Model: Linear probability, Method: OLS

(with heteroskedasticity-robust t-values)

Equation	1		2		3		4	
Dependent variable: Full-time employment (sample size = 4,616)	Coefficient	t-value	Coefficient	t-value	Coefficient	t-value	Coefficient	t-value
Constant	0.784	28.955	0.797	29.514	0.786	28.480	0.780	28.336
Grad in 2009	-0.019	-2.220	-0.023	-2.698	-0.021	-2.404	-0.019	-2.263
Economics	-0.025	-1.195	-0.021	-1.012	-0.021	-1.004	-0.025	-1.186
Business	-0.039	-1.875	-0.033	-1.564	-0.030	-1.449	0.039	-1.879
Law	-0.030	-1.400	-0.029	-1.333	-0.026	-1.189	-0.030	-1.382
Languages	-0.076	-3.183	-0.067	-2.815	-0.067	-2.804	-0.073	-3.083
Culture	-0.075	-2.923	-0.080	-3.073	-0.072	-2.793	-0.078	-3.023
Science	-0.072	-2.491	-0.076	-2.638	-0.071	-2.465	-0.070	-2.500
Male/Female	0.025	2.351	0.023	2.199	0.020	1.878	0.025	2.390
GPA1	0.039	4.421	0.040	4.528	0.041	4.710	0.038	4.328
GPA3	0.035	4.078	0.033	3.804	0.036	4.202	0.033	3.819
Career	0.019	5.816						
WIL			0.056	6.389			0.076	7.190
Induction					0.018	2.085	0.037	3.877
Adjusted R²	0.033		0.031		0.028		0.035	
F-statistic	15.099		14.613		13.097		14.811	
Prob(F-statistic)	0.000		0.000		0.000		0.000	

Table 10-2B Determining factors of employment outcome by company status

Model: Linear probability, Method: OLS   (with heteroskedasticity-robust t-values)

Dependent variable: Listed Company (sample size = 3,965)

Equation	1		2		3		4	
	Coefficient	t-value	Coefficient	t-value	Coefficient	t-value	Coefficient	t-value
Constant	0.247	4.882	0.260	5.139	0.258	5.028	0.254	4.959
Grad in 2009	−0.010	−0.650	−0.014	−0.954	−0.014	−0.911	−0.013	−0.856
Economics	−0.001	−0.021	0.003	0.076	0.041	0.096	0.002	0.050
Business	0.030	0.696	0.038	0.894	0.041	0.957	0.036	0.844
Law	−0.022	−0.518	−0.019	−0.445	−0.017	−0.401	−0.020	−0.456
Languages	−0.106	−2.375	−0.096	−2.142	−0.094	−2.104	−0.098	−2.187
Culture	−0.065	−1.385	−0.068	−1.431	−0.064	−1.351	−0.067	−1.418
Science	0.004	0.067	−0.001	−0.220	0.000	0.007	0.001	0.016
Male/Female	0.027	1.472	0.024	1.291	0.021	1.169	0.024	1.328
GPA1	0.009	0.597	0.010	0.730	0.012	0.810	0.010	0.684
GPA3	0.031	2.167	0.030	2.084	0.032	2.214	0.030	2.085
Career	0.019	2.829						
WIL			0.033	1.504			0.041	1.709
Induction					0.002	0.131	0.014	0.816
Adjusted R^2	0.011		0.010		0.009		0.010	
F-statistic	5.081		4.536		4.321		4.212	
Prob(F-statistic)	0.000		0.000		0.000		0.000	

(Note)

Significant at 5%
Significant at 10%

a female candidate is based on the past experience or statistics that says female employees are more likely to quit than the male counterparts. There have been a series of amendments since its introduction in 1985 of the Equal Employment Opportunity Law but it seems the effect is yet to be seen as far as the graduate labour market is concerned.

Now turning to the variables of main interest, GPAs seem to be significant factors for obtaining a full-time job. Academically competent students with higher GPA1 and /or GPA3 do well for a job search and GPA1 seems to have a slightly bigger impact than GPA3 in all four equations, for example, 0.039 for GPA1 and 0.035 for GPA3 in Equation 1 of Table 10-2A. It seems to suggest that both the pre-university achievement and university achievement raise the full-time employment probability, thereby supporting Hypotheses II and VI respectively. As far as cooperative education is concerned, their effects are all positive and significant – for example, one more cooperative education course, that is NoCE, seems to raise the employment prospect by 1.9 per cent. And WIL is about twice as effective as Induction, that is 7.6 per cent and 3.7 per cent in Equation 4 of Table 10-2A. This confirms Hypothesis IV. Thus, for obtaining a full-time job, all of cooperative education, pre-university academic performance, and academic performance at university have positive and significant effects.

Table 10-2B is analogous to Table 10-2A except for the dependent variable. It is a company status rather than employment status. The results are similar but generally somewhat weaker for the significance levels of estimated coefficients and the validity of the whole equation expressed in terms of adjusted R^2 and F-values in all four equations. In terms of the hypotheses, Hypothesis IV was somehow supported, Hypothesis II was not supported, and Hypothesis VI was strongly supported. Therefore, for obtaining a job at a listed company, cooperative education is somewhat effective, academic performance at university plays an important role, but pre-university academic performance does not seem to matter.

(2)   Does cooperative education programme have positive effects on job performance?

Background

In 2011, Center of Research and Development for Co-operative Education (CRDCE) at KSU conducted by post questionnaires to 10,383 alumni who graduated in March of 2006, 2007, 2008, and 2009. The government fund was granted to KSU by Japan's Ministry of Education, Culture, Science and Technology (MEXT) for financing an employability project. These alumni mostly in their early 20's with up to 5 years of working experience were asked about their thoughts on the earlier student life, the present employment, and the relevance of soft skills they acquired at university to the present employment, and work attitude. A total of 1,353 alumni replied to the questionnaires, or a response rate of 13.0 per cent.

These data were matched with the data previously collected on the GPA academic performance, faculty affiliation, and gender of those alumni, to analyse statistically the effect of cooperative education on the present job experience. The statistical analysis is performed on just over 1,000 samples of graduates from 2007, 2008, and 2009, in a similar manner to the analysis described in the earlier chapters, with their attributes such as gender, faculty, GPA's, as well as cooperative education course attendance, including WIL and Induction.

This analysis differs from the analyses of the earlier chapters in two ways. First, the data are collected form those who are already working as opposed to students preparing to work. This has an advantage and a disadvantage. The advantage is that the responses are based on actual experience at workplace. To the extent that the realization of the benefit of education is a long-term process, it should capture the benefit more appropriately than employment status of the first job. The disadvantage is that as the time passes after graduation, many other factors arise to affect the alumni's responses. Unless the questionnaires can capture these factors appropriately, the power of estimation is likely to be reduced resulting in a low value of adjusted R^2 or an F-value. Nevertheless, the effectiveness of cooperative education on work career is what all the practitioners in this field would like to know and more so if the data can be collected years after rather than just after graduation.

Second, the questionnaires ask what they perceive rather than objective facts about the alumni, and these responses are used as dependent variables. One, therefore, has to bear in mind that what is produced as the empirical result has by and large an element of subjective evaluation of the respondents. What is investigated is whether the alumni are "satisfied" with educational service university has provided for working in society rather than whether educational service responds fully to social needs, although they are not unrelated. A similar study based on students' response has been done in Matsutaka, Tanaka, and Churton (2009), which looked at level of satisfaction on cooperative education by students. Out of those who graduated in 2006, over 1,300 students answered and a statistical analysis showed that the students felt making effort for academic studies did have a positive effect on job placement.

The details of the basic statistics and the questionnaires

The survey was conducted in order to evaluate the effect of KSU's cooperative education programme on the work careers of its alumni by CRDCE. The survey questionnaires were sent out by post on 31st of March 2011, and the replies received not later than 28th of April 2011 were used as valid data for the investigation. The subjects were 10,383 alumni who graduated between 2006 and 2009, and there were 1,353 valid replies with sampling response rate of 13.0 per cent (= 1,353/10,383).

The questions asked were of three types: (1) the employment situation since graduation up to the present and work attitude; (2) the usefulness of the cooperative education related courses taken at KSU in relation to work career since graduation; (3) free comments on the KSU's cooperative education programme. For (1) and (2), the respondents are asked to choose one out of 1~5 ranking – that is, strongly agree, agree, cannot say which, disagree, strongly disagree.

Table 10-3 The basic statistics

(1) Gender	
Male	60%
Female	40%
(2) Average number of working years	1.993
(3) Distribution of students by faculty	
Economics	19.0%
Business	19.7%
Law	25.3%
Languages	15.7%
Science	4.7%
Engineering	5.1%
Cultural Studies	10.5%
(4) Average GPA	
1st year	2.071
3rd year	2.067
(5) Career-oriented education courses	
Average number of career-oriented education courses taken	1.144
Students who took at least one work-integrated learning course	17.4%
Students who took at least one Induction course	57.2%

Table 10-3 shows the basic statistics for the sample alumni, which may be summarized as follows:

(i) There are slightly more male than female alumni.
(ii) The average number of working years is just below 2 years.
(iii) Non-science alumni (i.e. other than Science and Engineering) constitute about 90 per cent.
(iv) Average GPA's for first and third years were both just above 2.0.
(v) The average number of cooperative education related courses alumni took was just over 1.
(vi) Of the cooperative education related courses, WIL courses were taken by about one in every five to six alumni (17.4 per cent).
(vii) Of the cooperative education related courses, more introductory and non-WIL courses (i.e. Induction) were taken by about every other student.

Table 10-4 shows the questions asked and their responses, which are relevant to the present investigation. The five ranking responses for these questions were

Table 10-4 The summary of the responses to the questions (sample size = 1,005)

		Response
A.	About respondent status	
A1	Seminar member (% of respondents who participated in small seminar classes)	91.3%
A2	Full-time/Part-time (% of respondents who are at full-time jobs)	75.3%
A3	Duration of employment at the present job (by years)	2.222
A4	Desire to change the job (% of respondents who wish to change the present job)	29.4%
A5	Number of job changes since graduation	1.356
B.	About the present job [i]	
B1	I find the job rewarding.	69.2%
B2	I feel my pay is fair for what I do.	46.2%[ii]
B3	I feel I work too many days and hours.	55.6%[ii]
B4	Human relations at work is smooth.	76.6%
B5	My contribution is accessed properly.	59.5%
B6	My ability and aptitude fit well with my work.	46.4%[ii]
B7	Work burden and level are right for me.	48.4%[ii]
B8	I would like to develop my personality though this job.	74.2%
B9	I would like to continue this job as long as I can.	50.2%
B10	I am generally happy with the present job.	57.3%
C.	About skills acquired and improved though work [i]	
C1	Skill to deal with issues willingly	78.1%
C2	Skill to get others involved	63.3%
C3	Skill to set up a purpose and act accordingly	76.4%
C4	Skill to analyse a situation and verify its problems	73.9%
C5	Skill to clarify and prepare a process of problem solving	66.8%
C6	Skill to create new values	43.0%[ii]
C7	Skill to express own opinion to others	66.1%
C8	Skill to listen to opinions of others carefully	80.8%
C9	Skill to understand different opinions and positions of others	79.8%
C10	Skill to understand interactive relations with others and surroundings	80.4%
C11	Skill to follow social rules and stick by personal commitment	81.5%
C12	Skill to cope with cause of stress	55.3%
D.	About attitude towards work [i]	
D1	Long-term employment is a good thing.	61.2%
D2	Job satisfaction is more important than salary or other conditions.	50.7%
D3	Job is a means of self-realization.	54.8%

(*Continued*)

Table 10-4 (Continued)

		Response
D4	I have a clear future life plan.	39.2%[ii]
D5	Promotion is an important aspect of job.	65.3%
D6	I prefer to set up own business and be self-employed.	18.5%[ii]
D7	I would work in an environment where I can feel my contribution.	82.7%
D8	It is important to build up personal networks inside and outside workplace.	87.6%
D9	Human relation skills are becoming more important.	94.3%
D10	It is necessary to acquire actively skills necessary for performing jobs.	94.3%

Note:
  (i) the 1~5 ranking of strongly agree, agree, neither, disagree, strongly disagree were divided to 1 if strongly agree or agree and 0 otherwise.
 (ii) the question with more negative than positive response.

divided into 1 if "strongly agree" and "agree" and 0 otherwise, to create a binary data and the percentages of those who answered 1 are given by percentages. The result may be summarized as follows:

   (i) Most of alumni participated in "seminars," which is a small class with between 10 and 20 students that continues from second to fourth year (Question A1).
  (ii) The ratio of full-time to part-time employees is about 3 to 1 (Question A2).
 (iii) One in three to four alumni wishes to change the job (Question A4).
  (iv) The level of satisfaction of the present job (Category B) is relatively high, with some exceptions of pay, working days and hours, job fit, and work load and work level (marked with [ii]).
   (v) As for the skills acquired through working experience (Category C), the skill to create new values is the only skill less than a half of the respondents included (marked with [ii]).
  (vi) Among the attitudes to work (Category D), having a clear future plan, wanting to start own business, scored low (marked with [ii]).

The results of the regression analysis

The multiple regression analysis is employed to determine what cause the alumni's responses summarized in Table 10-4. A series of binary response models based on a linear probability model are estimated with OLS, where the dependent variables are those binary responses (RESP) of Table 10-4, and the independent variables are the alumni's attributes. The estimated equation based on Equation III, that is (7-3)" is linear because only the linear probability model is employed:

$$\text{RESP} = a3 + b3\ \text{GPA3} + c3\text{CE} + d3\text{GPA1} + m3\text{Faculty}$$
$$+ n3\text{Gender} + p3\text{WorkYrs} + q3\text{Zemi} + u3 \qquad (10\text{-}3)$$

with CE defined by WIL, Induction, or NoCE (See definition of the variables in Table 10-5).

Table 10-6 summarizes the main regression analysis results, and nine equations that show F-values with a 5 per cent significance level are listed. As in the earlier estimation results with a binary dependent variable, the adjusted R^2 are generally low, suggesting that there may be important variables missing. However, the F-values and certain variables with significance levels support the validity of the results. The sample size varies depending on the question as not everyone answered all the questions but generally is in the range of 800 to

Table 10-5 The definitions of variables in the regressions

A. Dependent variables (See Table 10-4 for the definitions)

B. Independent variables

Name	Description	Value
a3	Constant	
Gender	Gender	1 if male and 0 if female
WorkYrs	Number of working years since graduation	Cardinal value
Faculty dummy variables (Faculty of Engineering as the base group)		
E	Faculty of Economics	1 if Economics and 0 otherwise
B	Faculty of Business	1 if Business and 0 otherwise
J	Faculty of Law	1 if Law and 0 otherwise
L	Faculty of Foreign Languages	1 if Foreign Languages and 0 otherwise
S	Faculty of Science	1 if Science and 0 otherwise
C01	Faculty of Cultural Studies (Faculty of Engineering as the reference category)	1 if Cultural Studies and 0 otherwise
GPA1	GPA in the 1st year	Cardinal value
GPA3	GPA in the 3rd year	Cardinal value
WIL	Work-integrated learning course	1 if taken any and 0 otherwise
Induction	Inductive course	1 if taken any and 0 otherwise
NoCE	Number of career-oriented courses taken	
Zemi	Participation in a small class	1 if taken any and 0 otherwise

Table 10-6 The regression results

Model: A linear probability model, Method: OLS with heteroskedacity-robust t-values

(Equation 1)
Dependent variable: QA2 Full-time/Part-time
Included observations: 1,005

Variable	Coef.	t-value	P-value
C	0.309	3.055	0.002
Gender	0.091	2.854	0.004**
WorkYrs	0.062	3.707	0.000**
E	0.053	0.805	0.421
B	0.096	1.472	0.141
J	0.044	0.673	0.501
L	-0.013	-0.174	0.862
S	-0.120	-1.322	0.187
C01	-0.033	-0.431	0.667
GPA1	0.033	1.321	0.187
GPA3	0.004	0.173	0.863
WIL	0.091	2.805	0.005*
Zemi	0.158	2.817	0.005**
Adjusted R-squared	0.046		
F-statistic	5.023		
Prob(F-statistic)	0.000		

(Equation 2)
Dependent variable: QA4 Number of jobs
Included observations: 994

Variable	Coef.	t-value	P-value
C	1.184	6.490	0.000
Gender	0.067	1.165	0.244
WorkYrs	0.081	2.560	0.011*
E	0.029	0.294	0.769
B	0.053	0.512	0.609
J	0.182	1.751	0.080
L	0.299	2.491	0.013*
S	0.002	0.012	0.990
C01	0.258	2.091	0.037+
GPA1	0.018	0.398	0.691
GPA3	-0.022	-0.600	0.549
Induction	0.002	0.047	0.962
Zemi	-0.173	-1.516	0.130
Adjusted R-squared	0.016		
F-statistic	2.363		
Prob(F-statistic)	0.005		

(Equation 3)
Dependent variable: QB9 Like to continue the job
Included observations: 892

Variable	Coef.	t-value	P-value
C	0.468	3.809	0.000
Gender	0.040	1.010	0.313
WorkYrs	0.002	0.090	0.928
E	0.056	0.657	0.511
B	0.068	0.803	0.422
J	0.134	1.620	0.106
L	-0.010	-0.110	0.912
S	0.101	0.916	0.360
C01	-0.036	-0.388	0.698
GPA1	0.037	1.236	0.217
GPA3	-0.054	-2.068	0.039*
WIL	0.081	1.815	0.070+
Zemi	-0.033	-0.515	0.607
Adjusted R-squared	0.012		
F-statistic	1.934		
Prob(F-statistic)	0.027		

(Equation 4)				(Equation 5)				(Equation 6)			
Dependent variable: QB9 Like to continue the job				Dependent variable: QC7 Skill to express own opinion				Dependent variable: QC12 Skill to cope with stress			
Included observations: 892				Included observations: 997				Included observations: 997			
Variable	Coef.	t-value	P-value	Variable	Coef.	t-value	P-value	Variable	Coef.	t-value	P-value
C	0.459	3.741	0.000	C	0.300	2.742	0.006	C	0.387	3.417	0.001
Gender	0.039	0.978	0.329	Gender	0.046	1.319	0.187	Gender	-0.053	-1.456	0.146
WorkYrs	0.005	0.257	0.797	WorkYrs	0.061	3.334	0.001**	WorkYrs	0.058	2.983	0.003**
E	0.047	0.548	0.584	E	0.096	1.224	0.221	E	0.080	0.993	0.321
B	0.054	0.624	0.533	B	0.142	1.838	0.066+	B	0.126	1.556	0.120
J	0.127	1.527	0.127	J	0.086	1.125	0.261	J	0.058	0.737	0.461
L	-0.028	-0.308	0.758	L	0.174	2.181	0.030*	L	0.092	1.100	0.272
S	0.106	0.954	0.340	S	0.089	0.909	0.364	S	0.123	1.189	0.235
C01	-0.042	-0.453	0.651	C01	0.133	1.574	0.116	C01	0.170	1.953	0.051+
GPA1	0.036	1.190	0.234	GPA1	0.053	2.005	0.045*	GPA1	-0.013	-0.453	0.651
GPA3	-0.052	-1.984	0.048*	GPA3	-0.048	-2.253	0.025*	GPA3	-0.004	-0.164	0.870
NoCE	0.029	2.080	0.038*	WIL	0.026	0.658	0.511	NoCE	0.027	2.151	0.032*
Zemi	-0.042	-0.649	0.516	Zemi	0.096	1.687	0.092+	Zemi	-0.002	-0.042	0.966
Adjusted R-squared	0.014			Adjusted R-squared	0.019			Adjusted R-squared	0.013		
F-statistic	2.017			F-statistic	2.611			F-statistic	2.058		
Prob(F-statistic)	0.020			Prob(F-statistic)	0.002			Prob(F-statistic)	0.017		

(Continued)

Table 10-6 (Continued)

	(Equation 7) Dependent variable: QD5 Promotion as important			(Equation 8) Dependent variable: QD6 Set up own business			(Equation 9) Dependent variable: QD10 Need to acquire skills		
	Included observations: 994			Included observations: 993			Included observations: 995		
Variable	Coef.	t-value	P-value	Variable	Coef.	t-value	P-value	Variable	Coef.	t-value	P-value
C	0.712	6.844	0.000	C	0.206	2.170	0.030	C	0.906	14.920	0.000
Gender	0.189	5.442	0.000**	Gender	0.111	4.072	0.000**	Gender	-0.020	-1.261	0.208
WorkYrs	-0.035	-1.983	0.048*	WorkYrs	0.000	0.018	0.986	WorkYrs	-0.007	-0.861	0.389
E	0.004	0.061	0.951	E	-0.015	-0.226	0.821	E	0.041	0.975	0.330
B	0.089	1.271	0.204	B	-0.032	-0.475	0.635	B	0.020	0.461	0.645
J	0.015	0.212	0.833	J	-0.116	-1.783	0.075+	J	0.065	1.630	0.103
L	0.013	0.175	0.861	L	-0.007	-0.108	0.914	L	0.032	0.754	0.451
S	0.002	0.026	0.980	S	-0.088	-1.061	0.289	S	-0.044	-0.697	0.486
C01	0.018	0.228	0.820	C01	-0.052	-0.751	0.453	C01	0.028	0.662	0.508
GPA1	-0.043	-1.627	0.104	GPA1	-0.009	-0.369	0.713	GPA1	-0.004	-0.389	0.697
GPA3	-0.061	-2.555	0.011*	GPA3	-0.027	-1.359	0.174	GPA3	0.021	2.066	0.039*
WIL	-0.069	-1.670	0.095+	WIL	-0.009	-0.292	0.770	WIL	0.007	0.440	0.660
Zemi	0.116	2.072	0.039*	Zemi	0.042	0.931	0.352	Zemi	0.004	0.143	0.886
Adjusted R-squared	0.070			Adjusted R-squared	0.022			Adjusted R-squared	0.011		
F-statistic	7.233			F-statistic	2.861			F-statistic	1.900		
Prob(F-statistic)	0.000			Prob(F-statistic)	0.001			Prob(F-statistic)	0.031		

** = significant at 1%, * = significant at 5%, + = significant at 10%

1,000. Some notable observations about the independent variables are listed below.

(i) Gender (1 if male) appears as a significant variable in several equations, that is Equations 1, 7, and 8. Male alumni tend to want to take initiatives at work by working full-time (Equation 1), being eager to be promoted (Equation 7), or even wanting to start up a new company (Equation 8).

(ii) Working more years (WorkYrs) appears as a significant variable Equations 1, 2, 5, 6, and 7. The significance in Equation 1 seems to suggest a movement from a part-time job to a full-time job. The significance in Equation 2 is obvious as you work more years, you are likely to have a more and not less number of jobs. The significant coefficients in Equations 5 and 6 imply that through years of working, skills to express one's opinion and cope with stress are acquired. What is interesting is its negative significance in Equation 7. This states that promotion becomes less important aspect in working life as one works more years. This may be because through experience one finds work to be collaborative activity rather than competition.

(iii) Multiple faculty dummies (E, B, J, L, S, and C01) show significance for Equations 2, 5, 6 and 8, but with no particular pattern. Graduates of Foreign Languages Faculty seem to change jobs more often (Equation 2) and to learn how to express one's opinion through work (Equation 5). Graduates of Cultural Studies Faculty seem to find how to cope with stress (Equation 6). And graduates of Law Faculty prefer not keen on setting up one's own business (Equation 8). Note that these results are all with respect to the faculty of engineering as the reference category. All they seem to suggest that there are faculty differences, but it needs a more extended investigation to determine the reasons behind these results.

(iv) As for GPAs (GPA1 and GPA3), GPA for third year seems to be a more significant variable. See Equations 3, 4, 5, 7, and 9. What is interesting is the signs of the estimates in these equations except for Equation 9 are all negative, giving a rather negative feeling towards the job and the acquired skills. One might interpret these results as alumni with high academic achievement finding the gap between the academic life and working life more difficult to close than those with lower academic achievement. It could be that for the high academic achievers working life is not as logical and fair as university studies. As for GPA1, its effect into employment seems to fade away unlike for GPA3 – university matters more than high school for life after graduation.

The result for participation in small and intensive class, that is, Seminar (or *Zemi* in Japanese), WIL, Induction courses (Induction), and a number of cooperative education related courses (NoCE) are the variables of the main interest for the present investigation.

(v) Participation in small class experience (Zemi) is a significant variable for Equations 1, 5, and 7. Equation 1 suggests that it helps obtaining a full-time job, while Equations 5 and 7 seem to suggest that the alumni find it comfortable to work in the organization if they have participated in small classes.

(vi) Induction generates no significant coefficient, implying basic or introductory courses in cooperative education do little for work career at least directly.

(vii) The number of cooperative education courses (NoCE) is a positive and significant variable in Equations 4 and 6. Equation 4 states that experience in cooperative education courses raises attachment to the present job, while Equation 6 states with these courses one can learn to cope with stress through work.

(viii) WIL appears as significant variable in Equations 1, 3, and 7. As it might have been expected, it acts positively in Equations 1 and 3 – Experience with WIL earns a full-time job and gives more attachment to the job. The negative sign in 7 seems to suggest that WIL helps students have a long-term perspectives about work career than mere promotion.

Conclusion

The main result of the investigation in this section may be summarized as follows. Cooperative education courses in general and WIL in particular seem to help students prepare well for their working life through having more realistic view about working. Small class participation, too, seems to prepare students for working in a group through close interactions with the tutor as well as fellow students. On the other hand, students with high GPA seem to feel less happy about work. This may be caused by finding a gap between academic studies and working life.

There are at least three lessons to be learned for the practitioners and the investigators. First, each faculty should clarify the range of skills they wish to offer and plan the academic programme accordingly. This lesson comes from the result that there is a faculty difference in response to the questionnaires. Second, the practitioners and investigators can rest assured that cooperative education and WIL in particular are effective tools for smooth transition from study to work. They seem to help students build an objective understanding about working life. Third, cooperative education is particularly useful for students with high academic achievement, who tend to find it difficult to adjust to working environment. This is more so as the other effective variable Zemi has already reached high level of participation (91.3 per cent in Table 10-4).

In terms of the hypotheses, this analysis proves that in a long run both cooperative education and university academic performance have a positive effect on employment outcome (i.e. Hypothesis IV and Hypothesis VI, respectively), while pre-university academic performance does not (i.e. Hypothesis II does not hold).

The estimation results in this chapter may be summarized as follows in terms of the hypotheses IV, II, and VI. Hypothesis IV is supported strongly with a full-time job status and to a certain extent with a listed company status. From the alumni data, too, it seems to give a positive effect and thus also supporting the Hypothesis IV. Hypothesis II is strongly supported with a full-time job status, but not with a listed company status or at work. From the alumni data, the effect almost disappears. Hypothesis VI is strongly supported with a full-time job status, a listed company status, but it has a negative effect on the performance of alumni and at work. On the whole, university and its cooperative education practitioners will be relieved to hear that their work has positive effects on students' job in an immediate as well as medium-term prospects.

11 Conclusion

The book focused on cooperative education as a new type of educational programme to answer to the needs of industrial societies with a large population of educated labour force. As explained in Part I, the history of cooperative education started more than a century ago in the United States, but similar types of educational systems have also been developed in other countries. Yet, its development is slow, and it should receive more global popularity. In the American case, it lost the momentum for a while when the government support was reduced in 1990s. It is a labour intensive and thus costly programme, and thus understanding and support of the community at large is essential. It also needs more support from within the educational institutions, since some suspect this programme has a negative effect on other academic programmes. This book attempts to provide the practitioners of cooperative education a tool to prove the effectiveness of this educational programme both at university and workplace.

In Part II, economic analysis was employed to describe the functions of cooperative education. It was argued that cooperative education can play the same role as the academic programme for forming human capital and signalling at university as well as OJT at workplace. Furthermore, its effectiveness for human capital formation and signalling may be superior as the programme offers an interaction of study and work in the industrial societies where university graduates form a large part of its labour force. The Japanese case illustrated how the development of cooperative education could interact with its socioeconomic environment.

In Part III, statistical and econometric tools were introduced to identify the effectiveness of cooperative education. For statistical tools, a z test and a χ^2 test was used for a comparison of two averages and z test and an analysis of variance (ANOVA) were used for a comparison of two proportions. Using the Kyoto Sangyo University (KSU) data, the tests showed that the first year and third year GPAs as well as proportion of students with full-time job were all significantly higher for students with cooperative education, while no clear result was obtained for company status. But it was suspected that the effectiveness of cooperative education might be somewhat overestimated as coop students were also found to be academically competent students.

In order to clarify this doubt, econometric tools were used with path analysis and multiple regression models to test the causal relationships among the factors in terms of six hypotheses. This was done by using the KSU and Hong Kong Polytechnic University (PolyU) student data and the main results of the econometric estimation imply that the following hypotheses hold:

Hypothesis I: Pre-university academic performance *positively* affects cooperative education participation.

Hypothesis II: Pre-university academic performance *positively* affects employment outcome.

Hypothesis III: Pre-university academic performance *positively* affects academic performance at university.

Hypothesis IV: Cooperative education *positively* affects employment outcome.

Hypothesis V: Cooperative education *positively* affects academic performance at university.

Hypothesis VI: Academic performance at university *positively* affects employment outcome.

which suggest the positive effects on cooperative education on academic performance and employment outcome. It is important to point out, however, that these hypotheses were tested and accepted based on a particular set of data, that is, of KSU and PolyU. It would require a set of data that includes a variety of institutions to correctly test these hypotheses as a general rule. Nevertheless, some common results obtained from the KSU and PolyU data seem to suggest that the general rule may not be too far from what our data derived. At least, the same approach can be employed to verify these hypotheses at the practitioner's own institution using own data set. This is good enough as a useful set of information to appeal to other academic staffs as well as the administration of the effectiveness of cooperative education. Or if the empirical result is not a favourable one, then it can always be used to revise the programme.

Following the concepts of earnings functions and internal rate of return (IRR) used in Chapter 3, one may be tempted to collect data on earnings that state whether cooperative education was taken. Together with other attributes such as age and gender, effect of cooperative education on earnings as well as IRR of cooperative education can be derived. This would attract more interest on the issue of cooperative education among labour economists. But for the time being, it requires more time and financial resources to accumulate the data.

As was stressed in the introduction, the book was written with the busy practitioners in mind, who cannot spare much time for going through throughly textbooks of labour economics, statistics, and econometrics. Thus, it is made as compact as possible without leaving out the essential logics behind the theoretical framework and quantitative analysis, so that any empirical investigation can be performed with a sound reasoning. Or for those interested in knowing more about the logics I have provided the reference alongside the topics. I hope my intention was successful.

Finally and once more, it is important to emphasize that this approach can identify how effective cooperative education is but cannot identify its process. This has to be solved by more qualitative investigation as opposed to the quantitative investigation of this book. This is not to say one approach is better than the other, but rather they need to be employed alongside. As much as cooperative education is a multidisciplinary field, so should its investigation be.

Bibliography

Addison, J. and Siebert, S. (1979): "The Market for Labor: An Analytical Treatment," Santa Monica, CA, Goodyear Publishing Company, Inc.

Arrow, K. (1973): "The Theory of Discrimination," in Ashenfelter, O. and Rees, A. (Eds.): "Discrimination in Labor Markets," Princeton, NJ, Princeton University Press.

Becker, G. (1957): "The Economics of Discrimination," Chicago: University of Chicago Press.

Becker, G. (1964): "Human Capital: A Theoretical and Empirical Analysis, with Special Reference to Education," New York, National Bureau of Economic Research distributed by Columbia University Press.

———. (1993): "Human Capital: A Theoretical and Empirical Analysis, with Special Reference to Education," 3rd Edition, Chicago, University of Chicago Press.

———. and Tomes, N. (1986): "Human Capital and the Rise and Fall of Families," *Journal of Labor Economics,* vol. 4: S1–S39.

Bedard, K. (2001): "Human Capital versus Signaling Models: University Access and High School Dropouts," *Journal of Political Economy,* vol. 109, no. 4, pp. 749–775.

Billet, S. and Choy, S. (2011): "Cooperative and Work-Integrated Education as a Pedagogy for Lifelong Learning," in Coll, R.K. and Zegwaard, K.E. (Eds.): "International Handbook for Cooperative and Work-Integrated Education," 2nd Edition, Lowell, MA, World Association for Cooperative Education, pp. 25–30.

Bjorklund, A., Jantti, M., and Solon, G. (2005): "Influences of Nature and Nurture on Earnings Variation: A Report on a Study of Various Sibling Types in Sweden," in Bowels, S., Gintis, H., and Osborne, M. (Eds.): "Unequal Chances: Family Background and Economic Success," Princeton, NJ, Princeton University Press.

Blalock, H.M. (1985): "Causal Models in the Social Sciences," 2nd Edition, New York, Aldine.

Blondal, S., Field, S., and Girouard, N. (2002): "Investment in Human Capital Through Upper-Secondary and Tertiary Education," *OECD Economic Studies,* no. 34, 2002/I, pp. 41–89.

Borjas, G.J. (2010): "Labor Economics," Gardner Press, 5th Edition, New York, McGraw-Hill International Edition.

Bouchard, T. and McGue, M. (1981): "Familial Studies of Intelligence," *Science,* vol. 250, pp. 223–228.

Bowles, S., Gintis, H., and Osborne, M. (2001): "Determinants of Earnings: A Behavioral Approach," *Journal of Economic Literature,* vol. 39, no. 4, pp. 1137–1176.

––––––. (2005): "Introduction," in Bowels, S., Gintis, H. and Osborne, M. (Eds.): "Unequal Chances: Family Background and Economic Success," Princeton, NJ, Princeton University Press.

Brimble, M., Freudenberg, B., Cameron, C., and English, D. (2011): "Professional Accounting Education – The WIL Experience," *Journal of Cooperative Education and Internships,* vol. 45, no. 01, pp. 80–92.

Brooks, C. (2008): "Introductory Econometrics for Finance," 2nd Edition, Cambridge, Cambridge University Press.

Committee on Education, House of Representatives, Sixty-third congress, United States of America (1914): "Cooperative System of Education – Vocational Education," in a hearing before the Committee on Education (second session) of Herman Schneider, on 26th of January 1914, Washington, Government Printing Office.

Conger, D. and Long, M.C. (2010): "Why are men falling behind? Gender gaps in college performance and persistence," *The Annals of the American Academy of Political and Social Science,* vol. 627, no. 1, pp. 184–214.

Cox, D.R. and Wermuth, N. (1992): "A Comment on the Coefficient of Determination for Binary Responses," *The American Statistician,* vol. 46, no.1, pp. 1–4.

Dewey, J. (1916): "Democracy of Education: An Introduction to the Philosophy of Education," New York, The Free Press.

––––––. (1938): "Experiennce and Education," New York: Collier Books.

Doeringer, P. and Piore, M. (1971): "Internal Labour Markets and Manpower Analysis," Lexington, MA, DC Heath.

Duckworth, A.L. and Seligman, M.E.P. (2006): "Self-discipline gives girls the edge: Gender in self-discipline, grades, and achievement test scores," *Journal of Educational Psychology,* vol. 98, pp. 198–208.

Duignan, J. (2003): "Placement and adding value to the academic performance of undergraduates: Reconfiguring the architecture – an empirical investigation," Journal of Vocational Education and Training, vol. 55, no. 3, pp. 335–350.

Duncan, G., Kalil, A., Mayer, S., Tepper, R., and Payne, M. (2005): "The Apple Does Not Fall Far from the Tree," in Bowels, S., Gintis, H. and Osborne, M. (Eds.): "Unequal Chances: Family Background and Economic Success," Princeton, NJ, Princeton University Press.

Eames, C. and Cates, C. (2011): "Theories of Learning in Cooperative and Work-Integrated Education," in Coll, R.K. and Zegwaard, K.E. (Eds.): "International handbook for cooperative and work-integrated education, 2nd Edition, Lowell, MA, World Association for Cooperative Education, pp. 41–52.

Feldman, M., Li, S., Li, N., Tuljapurkar, S., and Jin, X. (2005): "Son Preference, Marriage, and Intergenerational Transfer in Rural China," in Bowels, S., Gintis, H. and Osborne, M. (Eds.): "Unequal Chances: Family Background and Economic Success," Princeton, NJ, Princeton University Press.

Foster, H., Green, P., Houston, P., McAree, D., McCann, C., McCulloch, D., and Pogue, M. (2011): "Are sandwiches better? The impact of work placement upon degree performance," *Perspective on Pedagogy and Practice,* University of Ulster, vol. 2, pp. 53–64.

Gochenauer, P. and Winter, A. (2003). "Chapter 8: Analyzing Data With Statistics: Business Internship Effects on Postgraduate Employment," in Linn, P.L., Howard, A., and Miller, E. (Eds.): "Handbook for Research in Coop Education and Internships," New York, Routledge.

Goldberger, A.S. (1972): "Structural Equation Methods in the Social Sciences," *Econometrica*, vol. 40, no. 6, pp. 979–1001.

Gomez, S., Lush, D., and Clements, M. (2004): "Work placements enhance the academic performance of bioscience undergraduates," *Journal of Vocational Education and Training*, vol. 56 no. 3, pp. 373–386.

Greene, W.H. (2008): "Econometric Analysis," 6th Edition, Upper Saddle River, NJ, Pearson Prentice Hall.

Groenewald, T., Drysdale, M., Chiupka, C., and Johnson, N. (2011): "Towards a definition and models of practice for cooperative and work-integrated education," in Coll, R.K. and Zegwaard, K.E. (Eds.): "International Handbook for Cooperative and Work-Integrated Education," 2nd Edition, Lowell, MA, World Association for Cooperative Education.

Hartley, J.L. and Smith, B.W. (2000): "Strengthen academic ties by assessment of learning outcomes," *Journal of Cooperative Education*, vol. 35, no. 1, pp. 41–47.

Hertz, T. (2005): "Rags, Riches, and Race: The Intergenerational Economic Mobility of Black and White Families in the United States," in Bowels, S., Gintis, H., and Osborne, M. (Eds.): "Unequal Chances: Family Background and Economic Success," Princeton, NJ, Princeton University Press.

Heller, B. and Heinemann, H.N. (1987): "The impact of structured and non-structured work experiences on college students' attitude, values and academic performance," *Journal of Cooperative Education*, vol. 23, no. 3, pp. 19–32.

Ilmanen, A. (2003, winter): "Expected Returns on Stock and Bonds," *The Journal of Portfolio Management*, pp. 7–27.

Kaplan, D.W. (2000): "Structural Equation Modeling: Foundations and Extensions," Thousand Oaks, CA, Sage.

Kolb, D.A. (1984): "Experiential Learning: Experience as the source of learning and development," Engelwood Cliffs, NJ: Prentice Hall.

Krajcik, J.S. and Blumenfeld, P. (2006): " Project-based learning," in Sawyer, R.K. (Ed.), "The Cambridge Handbook of the Learning Sciences," New York, Cambridge.

Kroch, E. and Sjoblom, K. (1994): "Schooling as Human Capital or a Signal: Some Evidence," *Journal of Human Resources*, vol. XXXIX, pp. 156–180.

Lewin, K. (1946): "Action research and minority problems," *Journal of Social Issues*, vol. 2, no. 4, pp. 34–46.

Lleras, C. (2005): "Path Analysis," in Kempf-Leonard, K.L. (Ed.), "Encyclopedia of Social Measurement," Amsterdam, Elsevier Academic Press.

Loehlin, J. (2005): "Resemblance in Personality and Attitudes between Parents and Their Children: Genetic and Environmental Contributions," in Bowels, S., Gintis, H. and Osborne, M. (Eds.): "Unequal Chances: Family Background and Economic Success," Princeton, NJ, Princeton University Press.

Mandilaras, A. (2004): "Industrial placement and degree performance: Evidence from a British higher institution," *International Review of Economics Education*, vol. 3, no. 1, pp. 39–51.

Marini, R. and Tillman, R. (1998): "Giving graduates worldwide the business skills they need through cooperative education," *Journal of Cooperative Education and Internships*, vol. 33, no. 2, pp. 50–59.

Maruyama, G.M. (1997): "Basics of Structural Equation Modeling," Thousand Oaks, CA, Sage.

Matsutaka, M., Tanaka, Y., and Churton, P. (2009): "Assessing the effectiveness of co-op education in Japan: A panel data analysis at KSU," Paper presented at the 16th WACE World Conference, Vancouver.

Mazumder, B. (2005): "The Apple Falls Even Closer to the Tree than We Thought: New and Revised Estimates of the Intergenerational Inheritance of Earnings," in Bowels, S., Gintis, H. and Osborne, M. (Eds.): "Unequal Chances: Family Background and Economic Success," Princeton, NJ, Princeton University Press.

McFadden, D. (1974): "Conditional logit analysis of qualitative choice behavior," in P. Zarembka (Ed.): "Frontiers in Econometrics," New York: Academic Press, pp. 105–142

McNabb, R., Pal, S., and Sloane, P. (2002): "Gender Differences in Educational Attainment: The Case of University Students in England and Wales," *Economica,* vol. 69, pp. 481–503.

Mendez, R. (2008): "The correlation between industrial placements and final degree results: A study of Engineering Placement Students," Paper presented it the ASET conference, Plymouth.

Mendez, R. and Rona, A. (2010): "The Relationship between Industrial Placements and Final Degree Results: A Study of Engineering Placement Students," *Learning and Teaching in Higher Education,* Issue 4–2, pp. 46–61.

Mincer, J. (1974): "Schooling, experience, and earnings," New York, Columbia University Press.

Ministry of Education, Culture, Science and Technology (2009): "School Basic Survey," The Government of Japan.

Ministry of Education, Culture, Science and Technology, Japan (2013): "A report on internship practices at higher education institutions in 2011" [*Daigaku tou ni okeru heisei 23 nen no Internship jisshu jokyo ni tsuite* (in Japanese)], The Government of Japan.

Ministry of International Affairs and Communications: "Labour Force Survey," Annual Report, The Government of Japan.

Mulligan, C. (1997): "Parental Priorities and Economic Inequality," Chicago: University of Chicago Press.

Organization of Economic Cooperation and Development (2013): "Education at Glance." http://www.oecd.org/edu/eag2013%20(eng)--FINAL%2020%20 June%202013.pdf

Osborne, M. (2005): "Personality and the Intergenerational Transmission of Economic Status," in Bowels, S., Gintis, H., and Osborne, M. (Eds.): "Unequal Chances: Family Background and Economic Success," Princeton, NJ, Princeton University Press.

Ott, R. and Longnecker, M. (2010): "An Introduction to Statistical Methods and Data Analysis, International Edition," 6th Edition, Belmont, CA, Brooks/Cole, Cengage Learning.

Patrick, C.-J. and Kay, J. (2011): "Establishing a new nationwide network for promoting cooperative and work-integrated education," in Coll, R. K. and Zegwaard, K. E. (Eds.) "International Handbook for Cooperative and Work-Integrated Education," 2nd Edition, Lowell, MA, World Association for Cooperative Education, pp. 371–380.

Perlin, R. (2011): "Intern Nation: How to Earn Nothing and Learn Little in the Brave New Economy," London, Verso Books.

Phelps, E. (1972, September): "The Statistical Theory of Racism and Sexism," *American Economic Review,* vol. 62, pp. 659–661.

Piaget, J. (1985): "The equilibrium of cognitive structures," Chicago, University of Chicago Press.

Riley, J. (1979): "Testing the Educational Screening Hypothesis," *Journal of Political Economy*, vol. 87, no. 5, S227–S252.

Ryan, P. (2001, March): "The School-to-Work Transition: A Cross-National Perspective," *Journal of Economic Literature*, vol. XXXIX, pp. 34–92.

Ryder, K. G. (1987): "Social and Educational Roots," in Ryder, K. G. and Wilson, J.W. (Eds.): "Cooperative Education in a New Era," San Franscisco, Jossey-Bass Publishers, pp. 1–12.

Smith, A. (1976): "An enquiry into the Nature and Causes of the Wealth of Nations,"New York, Oxford University Press.

Smith, J. (1999): "Healthy Bodies and Thick Wallets: The Dual Relation between Health and Economic Status," *Journal of Economic Perspectives*, vol. 13, no. 2, pp. 145–166.

Spence, M. (1973): "Job Market Signalling," *Quarterly Journal of Economics*, vol. 87, no. 3, pp. 355–374.

Sovilla, E. S. and Varty, J.W. (2011): "Cooperative and Work-integrated Education in the US, Past and Present: Some Lessons Learned," in Coll, R. K. and Zegwaard, K. E. (Eds.), "International Handbook for Cooperative and Work-Integrated Education," 2nd Edition, Lowell, MA, World Association for Cooperative Education, pp. 3–15.

Swift, A. (2005): "Justice, Luck, and the Family: The Intergenerational Transmission of Economic Advantage from a Normative Perspective," in Bowels, S., Gintis, H. and Osborne, M. (Eds.): "Unequal Chances: Family Background and Economic Success," Princeton, NJ, Princeton University Press.

Tanaka, Y. (2012) : "Evaluating the Effects of Career-Oriented Education on Academic Performance and Employment Outcome – A Statistical Analysis Based on Students' Data," *Forum of Higher Education Research*, Kyoto Sangyo University, vol. 2, pp. 9–16.

Tanaka, Y. and Carlson, K. (2012): "An international comparison of the effects of work-integrated learning on academic performance: A statistical evaluation of WIL in Japan and Hong Kong," *Asia-Pacific Journal of Cooperative Education*, vol. 13, no. 2, pp. 77–88.

Taubman, P. (1976): "The Determinants of Earnings: Genetics, Family, and Other Environments; A Study of Male Twins," *American Economic Review*, vol. 66, no. 5, pp. 858–870.

Thurow, L. (1975): "Generating Inequality," New York, Basic Books.

Tunali, I. (1987): "Path Analysis," in Eatwell, J., Milgate, M., and Newman, P. (Eds.): "The New Palgrave: A Dictionary of Economics," London, Macmillan.

Turner, S.M. and Frederick, A. (1987): "Comparing Programs Worldwide," in Ryder, K. G. and Wilson, J.W. (Eds.): "Cooperative Education in a New Era," San Francisco, Jossey-Bass Publishers, pp. 45–77.

Van Gyn, G., Cutt, J., Loken, M., and Ricks, F. (1996): "Investigating the educational benefits of cooperative education: A longitudinal study," *Journal of Cooperative Education*, vol. 32, no. 2, pp. 70–85.

Venables, A., Tan, G., and Bellucci, E. (2009): "The impact of Learning in the Workplace Policy on differing ICT degrees," Refereed paper Presentation, 16th World Conference of WACE, Vancouver, Canada.

Wilson, J.W. (1987): "Contemporary Trends in the United States," in Ryder, K. G. and Wilson, J.W. (Eds.): "Cooperative Education in a New Era," San Francisco, Jossey-Bass Publishers, pp. 30–44.

—— and Lyons, E. H. (1961): "Work-study college programs; appraisal and report of the study of cooperative education," New York, Harper.

Wonnacott, T. H. and Wonnacott, R. J. (1990): "Introductory Statistics for Business and Economics (Wiley series in probability and mathematical statistics)," New York, John Wiley & Sons.

Wooldridge, J. M. (2009): "Introductory Econometrics," 4th Edition, Mason, OH, South Western.

——. (2010): "Econometric Analysis of Cross Section and Panel Data," Cambridge, MA, The MIT Press.

Wooldridge, R. L. (1987): "Factors Influencing Recent Growth and Expansion," in Ryder, K. G. and Wilson, J. W. (Eds.): "Cooperative Education in a New Era," San Francisco, Jossey-Bass Publishers, pp. 13–29.

Wolpin, K. (1977, December): "Education and Screening," *American Economic Review*, 67, pp. 949–958.

Wright, S. (1921): "Correlation and Causation," *Journal of Agricultural Research*, 20, pp. 557–585.

——. (1925): "Corn and Hog Correlations," Washington: U.S. Department of Agriculture Bulletin 1300.

——. (1934): "The Method of Path Coefficients," *Annals of Mathematical Statistics*, vol. 5, pp. 161–215.

Zegwaard, K. E. and McCurdy, S. (2008): "Value of work placements for students and its influence on student performance: Faculty perceptions," in Coll, R. K. and Hoskyn, K. (Eds.): "Proceedings from the Annual Conference for the New Zealand Association for Cooperative Education," New Plymouth, New Zealand.

Index

For Product Safety Concerns and Information please contact our EU
representative GPSR@taylorandfrancis.com
Taylor & Francis Verlag GmbH, Kaufingerstraße 24, 80331 München, Germany

www.ingramcontent.com/pod-product-compliance
Ingram Content Group UK Ltd.
Pitfield, Milton Keynes, MK11 3LW, UK
UKHW021826240425
457818UK00006B/97